P9-CFL-521

YOUR MARYLAND

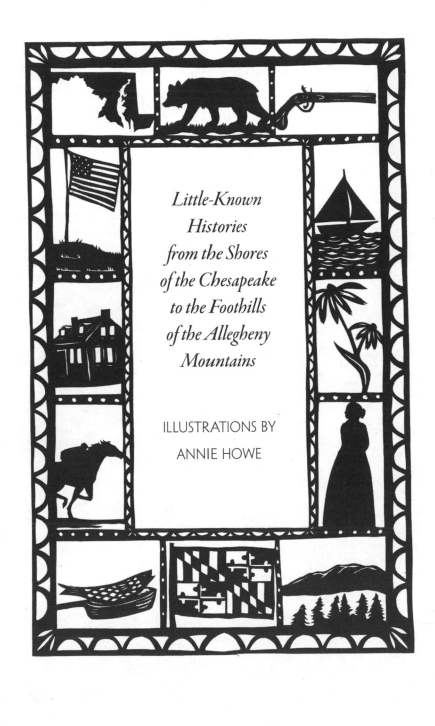

*Little-Known
Histories
from the Shores
of the Chesapeake
to the Foothills
of the Allegheny
Mountains*

ILLUSTRATIONS BY

ANNIE HOWE

RIC COTTOM YOUR
MARYLAND

JOHNS HOPKINS UNIVERSITY PRESS   *Baltimore*

© 2017 Ric Cottom
All rights reserved. Published 2017
Printed in the United States of America on acid-free paper
2 4 6 8 9 7 5 3 1

Johns Hopkins University Press
2715 North Charles Street
Baltimore, Maryland 21218-4363
www.press.jhu.edu

Library of Congress Cataloging-in-Publication Data
Names: Cottom, Ric, 1946–   author.
Title: Your Maryland : little-known histories from the shores of the
    Chesapeake to the foothills of the Allegheny Mountains / Ric Cottom.
Other titles: Your Maryland (Radio program)
Description: Baltimore : Johns Hopkins University Press, 2017. | Includes
    bibliographical references.
Identifiers: LCCN 2017008838| ISBN 9781421424057 (paperback :
    acid-free paper) | ISBN 9781421424064 (electronic) | ISBN
    1421424053 (paperback : acid-free paper) | ISBN 1421424061
    (electronic)
Subjects: LCSH: Maryland—History—Anecdotes. | Maryland—History,
    Local—Anecdotes. | Maryland—Biography—Anecdotes.
Classification: LCC F181.6 .C68 2017 | DDC 975.2—dc23
    LC record available at https://lccn.loc.gov/2017008838

A catalog record for this book is available from the British Library.

*Special discounts are available for bulk purchases of this book. For more informa-
tion, please contact Special Sales at 410-516-6936 or specialsales@press.jhu.edu.*

Johns Hopkins University Press uses environmentally friendly book materials,
including recycled text paper that is composed of at least 30 percent
post-consumer waste, whenever possible.

For June Matten Cottom,
who inspired
her son's love
of history

CONTENTS

[ix]

[xi]

PREFACE

Small as it is, Maryland has a long and colorful history, something I first became aware of when I arrived here from Pennsylvania more than four decades ago to study at Johns Hopkins University. That September, Baltimore was awash in orange and black, which soon gave way to blue and white, as the storied Orioles won the World Series and the Colts fought their way to the Lombardi Trophy.

The city was alive then, and still is. Sunlight glitters on the harbor that beckons one southward down the bay to the sea and adventure beyond. Cannon stare down from Federal Hill and peer solemnly across rocky fields near Sharpsburg, the Star-Spangled Banner floats over Fort McHenry, and a seventeenth-century English settlement arises out of an astounding archeological enterprise at Historic St. Mary's City. Annapolis preserves its colonial charm, watermen work the bay peacefully where once they fought oyster wars, Eastern Shoremen farm land that Frederick Douglass and Harriet Tubman knew, and Ellicott City rebuilds from a terrible flood— but one less catastrophic than that which roared down the Patapsco in 1868.

Twenty years ago, when I became editor of the *Maryland Historical Magazine*, with its circulation that surpassed many larger state journals, I saw at first hand how proud Marylanders were of their history and how eager many were to read and write about it. Nevertheless, most people regarded the Maryland Historical Society and its journal as a bit stodgy, a not entirely inaccurate assessment. How to change that? The answer presented itself one gray January day in 2002, when the society's director poked his head into my office and announced that Anthony Brandon, the new president of public radio station WYPR, wanted to include a number of short programs from local institutions in his lineup. Could we offer one? Well, yes. We could.

But how, exactly? Not long after I made my first attempts at writing for radio—with scripts that were too long and detailed—the answer came in a casual remark from one of the station's old hands. "Radio," he said, "is theater for the mind." And there it was. The scripts, though short, would have at their center a compelling human-interest story. That much was easy. Characters and ideas resided all about our editorial offices, in books that came in for review or perusal, in the library's historical manuscripts and photographs, in the histories we published at the Press at the Maryland Historical Society, and in the yards of shelf space containing a century of the *Maryland Historical Magazine*. Since we wanted to create mental images, all but the most basic elements had to be cast aside, allowing the script to move swiftly according to its new essentials: a background that told listeners where they were and when, and an arc with a beginning, middle, and end. Intonation and inflection could add color in place of additional explanation—all so that listeners might visualize what was going on during the drive home from work.

The result was and is *Your Maryland*, a series of short narrative histories that offer a look into the color and drama of

Maryland's history. Now in its fifteenth year, the program covers "nearly four centuries of heroes, scoundrels, floods, fires, riots, plots, athletes (two- and four-legged), beautiful spies, brilliant writers, misunderstood pirates, and ghosts." What follows is a representative selection. I hope you enjoy them as much as I have enjoyed crafting them.

YOUR MARYLAND

1

VOYAGE OF DISCOVERY

On June 2, 1608, Captain John Smith and fourteen men climbed into a thirty-four-foot boat and left the struggling Jamestown colony to explore the Chesapeake Bay. It was just the sort of thing Smith did best. Fearless, decisive, and bounding with energy, he also routinely bullied, lied, deceived, and brutalized anyone who got in his way.

At twenty-seven, Smith had already fought the Spanish and the Turks, been captured and sold into slavery in Istanbul, seduced a Turkish princess, and escaped back to Europe to fame and fortune. When he joined the first little fleet sailing for Virginia, though, other settlers found him so obnoxious they erected a gallows on deck to hang him. Then they opened their sealed orders for the colony's governance and learned he was one of seven chosen to lead them.

The fleet had no sooner arrived than Smith took over the place and promptly got himself in trouble with the Indians. Legend has it that he was saved by—what else? another princess, Pocahontas. But he returned to the settlement only to find the settlers ready to hang him again—that is, until he took over once more. Clearly, no one in Virginia was better qualified to lead an expedition up the Chesapeake than Captain John Smith.

On the eastern side of the bay, the expedition encountered friendly Indians and unfriendly weather. "The wind and waters so much increased with thunder, lightning, and raine," he said, that the sail blew overboard, "and such mighty waves overracked us" that only with great effort did they keep from sinking.

They could repair the sail with their shirts, but fresh water was hard to find, and as they proceeded, the Indians turned surly. Several hundred rushed to the shore and shot clouds of arrows at the boat, which Smith had prudently anchored just out of range. The next day the Indians returned and appeared more accommodating, so Smith blasted them with a volley of musketry that sent them scrambling for cover. He went ashore that night, quietly left some trinkets in their village, and waited until they came to terms.

Late in June he crossed the bay and reached about where the Bay Bridge is today, before turning south and exploring the Potomac. Several miles upriver he ran into three or four thousand Indians, "so strangely paynted, grimed, and disguised, shouting, yelling and crying as so many spirits from hell could not have shewed more terrible." Smith had his men fire low over the water so the Indians could see the skipping balls and hear the thunder of muskets echo from the heavily wooded shores. That impressed the Indians, who took Smith to a mine where they extracted the silvery powder with which they painted themselves so that they looked, he said, like "Blackmoores dusted over with silver."

Back in the boat, the explorers found fish "lying so thicke with their heads above the water" that for want of nets they tried to scoop them up with a frying pan. "Neither better fish, more plenty, nor more variety . . . , had any of us ever seene in any place," Smith remarked, "but they are not to be caught with a frying pan." Through crystal clear water the men could see large oysters littering the bottom like stones.

Smith amused himself by spearing fish with his sword. When he speared a ray, she suddenly struck him "with a most poisoned sting, of two or three inches long, bearded like a saw on each side." The barb went deep into his wrist, leaving a small hole that didn't bleed but did turn blue and radiated excruciating pain. Four hours later his arm had swollen horribly as high as his shoulder. Smith was directing his own funeral preparations when the party's doctor stuck a probe covered with a "precious oil" into the little blue hole. Miraculously, the swelling went down. Smith ate the ray for dinner.

The expedition returned to Jamestown on July 21. Smith decked the boat out with colors and ribbons, and he and his men regaled the colonists with tall tales until it appeared he had taken the whole of the Chesapeake by conquest. But the colonists—hungry, sickly, bickering, and resentful—weren't listening. Smith sighed and once more deposed the president and took control. Three days later he was back in his element, his little boat and sturdy crew headed north into the great bay of Chesapeake before him.

Sources: Susan Schmidt, *Landfall along the Chesapeake: In the Wake of Captain John Smith* (Baltimore: Johns Hopkins University Press, 2006). Quotes from Smith can be found in his journals, online at www.john smith400.org/journalfirstvoyage.htm.

2

AVALON

Every year, on March 25, we celebrate Maryland Day, the day in 1634 when the first settlers aboard the *Ark* and the *Dove* gave thanks for safe passage across the Atlantic and established "Maryland" on St. Clement's Island, near St. Mary's City. But Maryland might never have happened at all if George Calvert, the colony's founder, had originally had his way.

Calvert's father, Leonard, was a member of the lower gentry with a small estate in Yorkshire. He also leaned toward Catholicism, as did his more militant wife, Ann. Sixteenth-century England was a rough place to be a Catholic, and nowhere was that more true than in Yorkshire. Henry VIII had brutally clubbed down a Catholic uprising there, and Catholics everywhere were under suspicion. Leonard and his wife refused to take communion in the Anglican Church for as long as possible, but young George learned from the trouble they brought on themselves.

As he went through Trinity College, Oxford, studied law at the Inns of Court, and traveled across Europe, he accommodated himself to the prevailing winds. A bright and charming young man, he caught the attention of the king's officers and rose quickly to the highest office, secretary of state.

There he handled the most delicate problems—recovering jewels pawned by the king's nineteen-year-old daughter, for example—and stepped lightly across the quicksand of court politics while his wealth and power increased. Then in 1623 he misstepped, backing the marriage of Prince Charles to one of the Spanish Infantas. Had the marriage taken place, it might have lightened the burden on English Catholics. But the idea failed, and with it went Calvert's power at court.

Though by now Calvert had an estate in Ireland, he needed more money. Twenty years earlier, he had bought shares in the East India Company, then in the Virginia Company. The East India venture had paid well, but the idea of founding colonies for profit soon lost favor. In 1620, though, as the overseas boom was fading but while Calvert was still at the height of his power, he decided to exploit the rich fishing around Newfoundland. English fishermen had worked those waters for years, and promoters even claimed to have seen a mermaid. Starting a colony there seemed like a good idea. Calvert's first small party made it through the winter, and its leader, Captain Edward Wynne boasted, "The ayre here is very healthfull, . . . and the Winter short and tolerable, continuing onely in Ianuary, February, and part of March. . . . Neither was it so cold heere the last Winter as in England the yeere before." The settlement was in a province called "Avalon."

Several attempts to establish a colony failed when settlers succumbed to cold or scurvy, and in the summer of 1628 Calvert decided to go to Avalon himself. He took along most of his family, except for his oldest son, Cecil.

In Avalon he found not prospering settlers but marauding French pirates, pillaging the fishing fleets. The pirate captain, de la Rade, out of Dieppe, was capable and wily, but Calvert and his son Leonard outsailed and outwitted him, captured many of his ships, and chased off the rest. Yet victory was short-lived. As the colony headed into fall and winter, Calvert discovered what agents like Captain Wynne had hidden from him. "I haue fownd by too deare bought experience," he wrote the king, "that from the middest of October, to the middest of May there is a sadd face of winter upon all this land. . . . the ayre so intolerable cold as it is hardly to be endured." Calvert and half the hundred or so colonists fell ill. Nine or ten died.

Calvert gave up on Avalon and sailed for Virginia, thinking to spend his last days there, but the Virginians, being good Anglicans, wanted him to swear an oath that violated his Catholic principles. He refused and returned to England. His wife, leaving on another ship, died at sea. Not until June 1632 did King Charles grant Calvert another charter, this one for a settlement in the Chesapeake, but George Calvert never lived to see it. He died in April, leaving his son Cecil to carry on the venture, not in Newfoundland, Avalon, or Virginia, but in a place called Maryland.

Source: Thomas M. Coakley, "George Calvert and Newfoundland: The Sad Face of Winter," *Maryland Historical Magazine* 100 (2005): 7–28

3

THE MURDEROUS CAREER
OF JOHN DANDY

As your mother always told you, it's good to have a trade. Take the case of John Dandy, the gunsmith. In 1641, only three years after his arrival in St. Mary's City, he found himself sentenced to death. But Maryland needed a gunsmith, so acting governor Thomas Cornwaleys commuted his sentence to three years' service to the colony and had him set up shop inside the fort at St. Mary's.

Another three years passed, and another court found him guilty of assault against a young Indian boy named Edward. Dandy, the court said, had placed a "gonne charged with bullets against the said Edward did discharge & therewith did wound the said Edward in the right side of his belly near the navel, so that he pierced his gutts, of which . . . the said Edward . . . within the space of 3 days died." Dandy pled guilty, but his neighbors—who didn't like their odds in a colony without a gunsmith—asked for leniency. Governor Giles Brent sentenced Dandy to another seven years' service, and, sensing that he had a real talent on his hands, appointed Dandy public executioner.

In 1650, after a new governor had pardoned him for his past crimes, Dandy went after one Thomas Maidwell, who had apparently accepted some peaches from a young maid living in Dandy's house. Dandy was enraged, either because Maidwell was filching his peaches or because he was flirting with a girl Dandy had his eye on. Whatever the case, as Maidwell backpedaled to escape, Dandy's wife Ann snuck up from behind with an iron bar and staggered him with a blow to the head. Then Dandy hit him on the front of his head with a three-pound blacksmith's hammer. Somehow, Maidwell got to his feet and fled the shop. Somehow, too, the dispute was settled without criminal charges. Dandy had escaped once again.

In 1652, Governor Stone contemplated an expedition against the Indians. John Dandy made himself indispensable by fixing a number of guns and locks for the raiding party. That proved helpful a little later, when the Roman Catholic Dandy backed the losing side at the Battle of the Severn. Still in need of a gunsmith, a Puritan court let him off lightly with a fine of two thousand pounds of tobacco.

Then, in August 1657, luck finally ran out. While paddling his canoe past Dandy's mill, William Wood came upon the naked body of Dandy's young servant, Henry Gouge, floating in the creek.

Wood tied the boy's arm to his canoe and hauled the body ashore. He then brought the gunsmith and a couple of his men to look at it. John Dandy stood over the body, shook his head and muttered that "he should come to a great deal of trouble about this boy." An examination revealed a scar on the forehead and signs that Gouge had been beaten by a "small switch or rod."

For a time it looked like Dandy might dodge this one, too, but more people came forward. Servants told how they had heard poor Henry yelling "O Lord! O Lord!" around eleven that very morning, as Dandy beat him. Ann Dandy admitted that Henry Gouge had gotten the scar on his forehead when Dandy hit him with an axe handle back in June, and that at the time she had taken two pieces of Henry's skull out of the wound. Walter Peake claimed that the "poor lame boy" seemed to be much abused, with pinches around his ears. Then Richard Furbear, who lived in Dandy's house, mentioned that when John Dandy had examined Henry's body, the scar on Henry's forehead had oozed fresh blood. That did it. English forensic custom had it that when fresh blood appeared from a wound on the corpse, the murderer was at hand.

Dandy fled to Virginia, only to be recaptured and brought back to Maryland for trial. He protested his innocence, to no avail. This time there were no hostile Indians, and no war was imminent. Worse yet, the colony had acquired a second gunsmith. On October 3, 1657, they rowed John Dandy out to an island at the mouth of Leonard's Creek, and there, his volatile, murderous career came to an end—at the end of a rope.

Source: Information courtesy of Timothy B. Riordan, Historic St. Mary's City

4

WITCHCRAFT IN MARYLAND

In the spring of 1654, the good ship *Charity of London* was plowing across the icy North Atlantic, bound for Maryland, when she began to take on water. Crewmen tried to caulk the leaks, but the weather got worse, and her condition grew perilous. Desperately, the crew looked for the cause of their imminent sinking.

Among the passengers was a woman named Mary Lee. She was probably young and poor, perhaps one of the convict women given the choice of going jail or to Maryland and a life of fevers and hard labor. Maybe she had rejected a sailor's advances, or insulted the crew. Whatever the reason, they now accused her of being a witch.

The idea of witchcraft goes back to the beginnings of written history, and by the Age of Exploration, it was still a common belief. Witches gained their powers from consorting with the Devil and could cast a spell causing those they despised to become lame, or waste away. In 1489, two papal inquisitors codified the effort to find and execute witches into a single book, *Malleus Malificarum*, or "Hammer of Witches." One of its ideas, thought enlightened at the time, was that the Devil left his mark on witches, who were usually women.

Convinced they had a witch aboard the *Charity of London*, the crew went to Captain John Bosworth and demanded that he examine Mary Lee. Bosworth refused. He wouldn't take that upon himself, he said, but he would put Mary ashore on Bermuda. As luck would have it, the wind suddenly turned, making that impossible.

The crew now threatened to abandon ship if Mary were not examined. Bosworth tried to buy time. He told the crew that a trial would require that the masters of other ships be present, something the stormy weather would not permit.

The crew then took matters into their own hands. Two of them seized Mary, and, according to eyewitness accounts, "Searched her and found Some Signall or Marke of a witch upon her." They called the ship's master and others to see the mark, and tied Mary to the capstall between decks. In the morning the mark had largely disappeared, and the crew demanded another search. Realizing she had no chance, Mary confessed.

The crew demanded that she be hanged. Bosworth again refused and went to his cabin. Several of the crew followed and shouted that if he wouldn't give the order, they'd all do it themselves, everyone laying hands on her so no one person could be blamed. Bosworth slammed the cabin door in their faces. Shortly thereafter, the crew had its way, and on a leaking ship, in a gale-tossed sea, with all hands taking part, Mary Lee was hanged.

John Bosworth was not the only man of his time to be troubled at the idea of executing women for witchcraft. Many in Maryland shared his views, and as a result, there were only a handful of witchcraft trials in the province. Certainly, Maryland saw nothing like the panic that infected Salem, Massachusetts, where in just fourteen terrible months in 1692 and 1693, more than 160 people were accused of witchcraft, and at least twenty-five were executed or died in jail.

But Maryland was not completely free of witches. In 1685, Rebecca Fowler, a Calvert County planter's wife, was hanged for "being led by the . . . Divell [and practicing] certaine evil & dyabolicall artes called witchcrafts, inchantments charmes, & sorceryes . . . upon . . . one Francis Sandsbury & several others." Hannah Edwards barely escaped a similar fate the same year. In Talbot County, Virtue Violl was accused of rendering "the Tongue of . . . Elinor Moore . . . speechless." Violl was acquitted, and one can't help but wonder if perhaps Elinor Moore didn't deserve it. Sometimes accused witches turned the tables and sued the neighborhood gossips for slander. Often, they won.

All in all, early Marylanders seemed to agree with Joseph Addison, who wrote in the *Spectator* of London: "[I] believe in general that there is and has been such a thing as Witchcraft, but at the same time [I] can give no Credit to any Particular Instance of it." He wrote that early in the eighteenth century. Today, of course, we know better. Jack Nicholson charmed *The Witches of Eastwick*, and Wiccans practice their craft everywhere, we hope benevolently. So, if a happy little witch knocks on your front door in the next few days, give her some candy—just to be on the safe side.

Sources: Archives of Maryland, 3:306–8; Raphael Semmes, Crime and Punishment in Early Maryland (Baltimore: Johns Hopkins Press, 1938), 168–69

5

THE MONSTER

One of western Maryland's most notable figures—even before he went west—was Thomas Cresap. Short, stocky, and immensely powerful, he was a force of nature and so strong they said he never lost a fight or a test of strength. Born in 1694 to English yeomen in Yorkshire, the home of the Calvert family, he came to Maryland in his early twenties, fell into debt, and fled to Virginia to escape his creditors. Virginia didn't want him, either, so he returned to Maryland. In 1729 he moved from near Havre de Grace up the Susquehanna to what is now Wrightsville, Pennsylvania, where the governor of Maryland had granted him five hundred acres he called Pleasant Garden.

The land on which he had settled was very much in dispute between the Calverts and the sons of William Penn, who just then were arguing over their common boundary. Making matters worse was a tide of German immigrants moving westward into the region who did not know to whom they should pay taxes or express allegiance.

Thomas Cresap regarded himself first and foremost as a Marylander and set about clarifying matters. He soon found himself afoul of Pennsylvania law. When two Pennsylvanians ambushed him on the ferry he was operating, tried to drown him in the Susquehanna, and got away with it, Maryland made him a justice of the peace in Baltimore County and a captain in the militia, and sent him more men. Cresap's fortified house at Pleasant Garden became a strongpoint for raids on Pennsylvania German settlers. Anyone with allegiance to the Penns was fair game. If their horses or cattle broke into his corn, Cresap shot them. When the sheriff sent a posse to arrest him, Cresap shot at them, too, mortally wounding one man before driving the others off.

The Lancaster County sheriff had had more than enough. With a posse of almost thirty men—some said it was closer to fifty—he surrounded Cresap's house and ordered him to come out. Cresap refused. The sheriff shouted that he planned to burn the house, and at that one of Cresap's men escaped up the chimney. The others remained until flames forced them out. Cresap made a run for his ferry and might have escaped had he not tied the boat so securely. The posse fell upon him and bound his hands.

They had gotten halfway across the Susquehanna when Cresap elbowed one of his guards into the river. The others thought it was their prisoner and beat the man with their oars until they noticed that Cresap was still in the boat. He continued to amuse himself by annoying his captors all the way into Philadelphia. As the party entered the city, crowds came to see for themselves this man they called the "Maryland Monster." Sensing opportunity, Cresap turned to one of his guards, George Aston, and bellowed, "Damn it, Aston, this is one of the Prettyest Towns in Maryland!"

When they put him in irons, Cresap raised his arms and brought the shackles down on the blacksmith's head so hard the blow knocked him senseless. They threw him into prison and Maryland sent Daniel Dulaney and Edmund Jenings to argue his case. The proceedings dragged on, moving ever higher to the governors and provincial councils, and finally to the Crown. But the Pennsylvanians were losing their will. Thomas Cresap was making himself so obnoxious in their jail they couldn't stand him, but when they tried to release him, he wouldn't go, swearing he'd stay there until he got word from the king himself. Finally, the king ordered both sides to reconcile their border differences, and Cresap left Philadelphia.

Maryland lost the boundary dispute and had to settle for what is now the Mason-Dixon line. We can only wonder what would have happened had things gone differently and had Cresap prevailed. Philadelphia might indeed have become, one of the "Prettyest Towns in Maryland."

Source: Lawrence C. Wroth, "The Story of Thomas Cresap, a Maryland Pioneer," *Maryland Historical Magazine* 9 (1914): 1–35

6

THE BLOOD-RED FLAG

On April 23, 1700, the *Pennsylvania Merchant*, a ship of eighty tons out of London bound for Philadelphia, was nearing Cape Henlopen and the mouth of the Delaware Bay when her lookouts noticed a ship following them. It was late in the day, and nobody could make out who she was. The next morning, after an uneasy night, their worst fears were realized.

Bearing down on them was the pirate ship *La Paix*, "The Peace," a cruel name for a ship that just then was terrorizing the Chesapeake and Delaware Bays. Captain Louis Guillar called his large crew of French and Dutch pirates to quarters, ran out his twenty guns, and unfurled a huge "blood red flag," which struck terror in the hearts of the London merchantman. He called on the *Pennsylvania Merchant* to heave to, an order Captain Samuel Harrison quickly obeyed. The pirates rushed aboard, took everyone prisoner, rifled through their trunks, stole one man's watch, and seized everything of nautical value from the ship. Then they tore a hole in her side and set their prize on fire. Such was life in the Chesapeake in 1700.

The pirate Guillar had big plans. While he waited for friends aboard another small pirate vessel to join him, he seized ship after ship. He scuttled some but kept the more seaworthy to enlarge his fleet into something strong enough to handle the small warships England sent to protect the colonies. Thus when he spotted the formidable *Nicholson* just outside Lynnhaven Bay, bound for London, he boarded her. His men tossed a hundred casks of tobacco and other valuable cargo over the side to make room for cannons. Then they took her back to Lynnhaven harbor with four other prizes and set about making a fleet.

It so happened that on that Sunday afternoon, April 28, 1700, word reached Francis Nicholson, at his house nearby, that his namesake ship had been captured. Nicholson, a man of action who had recently been governor of Maryland and was now governor of Virginia, was entertaining several gentlemen. Among them was Captain William Passenger, commander of His Majesty's ship *Shoreham*, newly arrived to police the Chesapeake. Nicholson mobilized everyone in sight and ordered the *Shoreham* into Lynnhaven Bay to see about Guillar.

Captain Passenger was the right man for the job. By three the next morning the *Shoreham* was easing into Lynnhaven Bay. Guillar saw him coming. Using a bit of piratical guile, the Frenchman waited until the last minute, then suddenly hoisted sail and raced to gain the weather gauge. He intended to seize the wind, bear down on the *Shoreham*, and board her with his larger crew.

As the sun rose, out came that huge red flag. The next ten hours were like something straight out of *Master and Commander*, as the two captains jockeyed for position. Cannons roared. Rigging, sails, and masts were shot away. Screams and shouts pierced the rising wind. In the end, the *Shoreham* forced *La Paix* onto the shoals, where she couldn't maneuver. Guillar announced that he was going to blow up his ship with everyone on board, including his prisoners. One of those prisoners volunteered to swim to the *Shoreham* and negotiate a truce. He made it, and Captain Passenger generously assured

Guillar that he and his men would be given over to His Majesty's mercy and justice, which wasn't saying much but was the best Guillar was going to get. Guillar surrendered.

Colonial authorities hanged three of the pirates anyway, but the rest were put aboard the next convoy to London. When they inspected Guillar's ship, though, they found a surprise. There was plenty of powder and shot, and a few extra cannons on board, but provisions were pathetically meager. All Guillar had to feed 140 men and his prisoners was one barrel of beef, nineteen barrels of flour, two of which were musty, a few casks of bread, one cask of oatmeal, and three jars of oil. It turns out that beneath the blood-red flag that so terrorized Chesapeake shipping were men looking not for treasure, but for food. For such was life in the Chesapeake, in 1700.

Source: Henry F. Thompson, "A Pirate on the Chesapeake," *Maryland Historical Magazine* 1 (1906): 15–27

7

THE SUMMER OF '76

We tend to think of the summer of 1776 as a brilliant moment in American history. The Second Continental Congress had written the Declaration of Independence, and as couriers carried it throughout the thirteen colonies, cheering patriots picked up their muskets and got ready to throw off the yoke of George III.

But things weren't that simple in Maryland, which didn't instruct its delegates in Philadelphia to vote for independence until June 28, making it the last colony to do so. To the fiery Sons of Liberty in Baltimore, who were hell-bent on independence, it was high time. Earlier that spring they had sent Captain Sam Smith to Annapolis to seize the young, handsome, and popular royal governor, Robert Eden, only to be rebuffed by more conservative patriot leaders there.

They'd gone after Eden because some letters he had written to the governor of Virginia and to British officials had fallen into patriot hands. If war broke out, it wouldn't take much to keep Maryland in line, Eden said, a single British regiment ought to do it. At the end of June, the governor boarded a ship for England and home, but for a time it looked like Eden was right. No sooner was independence declared than fighting broke out between patriots and loyalists in Baltimore, and the Eastern Shore became a hotbed of support for the Crown.

In this confused and violent atmosphere, and frightened by the threat of revolution, Maryland's political leadership decided they had to form a new government. They set August 1 as the day to elect delegates to a convention that would create a new state constitution. Of course the next question was—who was going to vote, and the answer was, not everyone. A faction led by John Hall and Rezin Hammond called for an end to property restrictions on voting, so as to let the common man participate in government, but in the end, voting for convention delegates was limited to the well-off.

That summer the Continental Congress also authorized the recruitment of a body of soldiers from Pennsylvania, Delaware, and Maryland—ten thousand in all—to reinforce George Washington and his Continentals. The outfit was called the "Flying Camp," and the men in it were to serve until December 1, 1776. Maryland's quota was 3,405, and they quickly rushed to the colors.

As it happened, several companies of this "Flying Camp" reached Annapolis late in July and camped on a hill outside of town. August 1 came, and the soldiers, who had taken up arms to support a revolution that promised to create a democracy, asked where they might vote. The answer was that they weren't allowed to vote at all—they didn't meet the property qualifications. The men looked at one another in disbelief, then grew dangerously angry. Officers quickly moved in among them, persuading and demanding order. The soldiers eventually put down their weapons, but they never forgot the slight.

Eventually the troops marched out to join Washington's men in New York, but at the end of August the British surrounded and nearly destroyed the American army on Long Island. It was saved only when another regiment of Marylanders—

wealthy young men, landowners, and merchants' sons who had paid for their own weapons and uniforms—sacrificed themselves to save the army. Soon Washington was retreating through New Jersey, barely staying ahead of the British and desperately trying to keep his army from melting away. December 1 came, and the Flying Camp's enlistment expired. Would they remain with the army? The Marylanders among them said no and returned home, leaving Washington with barely three thousand men to carry on the war. A few of them thought about staying and fighting, like the Maryland regiment that had earned its glory on Long Island, but none of them did. They all returned home, many to join the large number of Marylanders who sat out the war on the sidelines. One wonders what they might have done, if, back in August, they had they been allowed to vote for the government they had been asked to die for.

Source: Ronald Hoffman, *A Spirit of Dissension: Economics, Politics, and the Revolution in Maryland* (Baltimore: Johns Hopkins University Press, 1973)

8

THE REVOLUTIONARY

As twilight fell on January 2, 1777, an outnumbered, ragtag army, many without shoes and shivering in the cold, gazed across Assunpink Creek on the edge of Trenton, New Jersey. The men nervously fingered their muskets and considered their situation, trapped as they were between the Delaware River and the British ranks marching steadily toward them. General Lord Charles Cornwallis was intent upon avenging the great embarrassment of eight days before, when George Washington had crossed the Delaware, overcome his Hessian mercenaries, and taken the town.

One of those men standing silently behind a cannon aimed across Assunpink Creek was a painter from Maryland named Charles Peale, now a lieutenant in the Philadelphia militia. How he came to be there is a story of the American Revolution.

Charles Willson Peale began life as one of several children born to a schoolmaster in Chestertown. When his father died, his mother took the impoverished family to Annapolis and apprenticed her son to a saddler, who took one look at the boy and thought he'd been swindled.

Yet Charles was strong for his size, a quick learner, and boundlessly energetic. As soon as his apprenticeship expired, he took a wife and set out on his own, working leather and also repairing clocks and watches. As a child he had acquired an interest in painting and thought now of earning money by painting portraits, but in trying to expand each of these talents into a business, he fell into debt. According to the law, a man who failed to repay a loan on demand went to prison until the debt was paid in full or his creditors let him out.

Like many another man in his position, young Peale naturally sympathized with the growing movement to make the government more democratic, and he took an active part in it, marching, organizing, and painting signs. That did not please the wealthy men who had lent him money and who decided to squelch him by suddenly demanding payment. Charles fled with his family to Queen Anne's County, but when the sheriff followed him there, he packed his painting supplies in a box one morning, mounted a horse named Gimlet, and galloped off to Virginia.

His brother-in-law, a ship captain, took him to Boston, where he sought out John Singleton Copley, Boston's greatest artist. Though irritated that Peale considered painting nothing more than a craft anyone could learn, Copley greatly improved the young man's technique. By the time Peale returned to Virginia, his portraits were impressive. A group of wealthy Annapolitans, led by Charles Carroll, the barrister, decided Maryland could use a good artist. They called off his creditors and raised the money to send this talented young man to London to study.

Reluctantly he went, abandoning his wife and children to work with the great Benjamin West. After two years, he returned to Annapolis and got out of debt by painting the portraits of the wealthy. One subject was the owner of Mount Vernon in Virginia, a towering, forty-year-old colonel named Washington, who slowly took a liking to him. When he had paid all his debts, Charles Peale bid farewell to the hard memory of Annapolis and his brush with debtor's prison, and moved north.

And so it came to be that the young portrait painter from Maryland stood with his company of Philadelphia militia and drove the British back from Assunpink Creek. The next day he was with them at the Battle of Princeton. The next winter, while the army suffered at Valley Forge, Peale slept out in the snowy woods nearby with a few of his fellow militiamen and used his knowledge of leather to make moccasins for the shoeless. To support his family, he painted miniatures—not of wealthy planters and merchants, but of the men of Valley Forge: George Washington, Nathanael Greene, Alexander Hamilton, Baron von Steuben, Henry Knox, "Mad" Anthony Wayne, Lafayette. With his quick brush and keen eye, the young apprentice from Annapolis, who had been hounded out of Maryland for falling into debt, became the next thing to the photographer of the American Revolution, leaving us on his canvases the determined faces of American independence.

Source: Robert Plate, *Charles Willson Peale: Son of Liberty, Father of Art and Science* (New York: David McKay, 1967)

9

PRIVATEERS

On January 23, 1778, in the dark days of the American Revolution, a young sailor from Dorcester County named John Kilby found himself in Portsmouth, England. Along with scores of other captured Chesapeake Bay mariners, he listened while a British magistrate condemned them all "for piracy and treason on his majesty's high seas." They *were* privateers, but as they marched off to jail, Kilby wondered just who had told His Majesty he owned the high seas.

That defiant spirit carried them through the slow rot that was life for Americans in Forton Prison, just outside Portsmouth. As "pirates," they received only two-thirds of the food ration for prisoners of war—a few ounces of scrap beef, a pint of broth, and every third day a loaf of bread and a little salt. The British had also bricked up the fireplaces in what had formerly been a hospital, so the men could enjoy an English winter with no heat.

In no time the Americans cut a hole in the ceiling, climbed into the garret, and chipped their way into the unused chimney. Using cords from their hammocks, they made a rope and lowered themselves as far as they could go, then began to tunnel their way out. Small groups of privateersmen began to surface here and there outside the walls.

One group had the bad luck to come up in the middle of a pig sty, whose occupants alerted the neighborhood. Almost all were recaptured and sentenced to forty days on bread and water in a place they called the "Black Hole." Their names were also put at the end of the list of men to be exchanged. But they never stopped trying to escape.

Finally, after twenty months, John Kilby's name was called for exchange. He and a hundred others formed up in the court-yard under guard and learned from the prison commander that His Majesty had now graciously pardoned them. The men shouted back, "Damn his majesty and his pardon, too!" As they marched out of the prison, they demanded that their guards play "Yankee Doodle," which, to cheers from the waving towns-people, the guards obligingly did. Passing the "Black Hole," they wished their friends good luck, only to have the punished men reply that they'd be in France first.

That's precisely what happened. When Kilby's group arrived in Nantes a few days later, who should meet them on the wharf but the men they'd left behind in the Black Hole. Some-how they'd broken out, made their way to the Portsmouth docks, quietly stolen a barge from among His Majesty's ships of the line riding in the harbor, and sailed to France.

Deciding it was high time they repaid their British jailers, thirty-three of the privateers applied to an American captain of growing reputation, named John Paul Jones, and signed on to serve with him on the *Bonhomme Richard*, just then fitting out in L'Orient. A few weeks later they were once again doing what they did best—raiding a British convoy and clearing for a fight with its escort, the heavily armed *Serapis*.

The two ships squared off and unleashed their broadsides at one another. Quarter gunner John Kilby, late of Dorchester County, did his part in bringing down the *Serapis's* rigging, but the British guns inflicted heavy damage on the *Richard's* hull, and she began taking on water. Both ships caught fire. Jones had his men throw grappling hooks at the *Serapis* so they could lash the two ships together, and told them not to worry, there was plenty of wood to float on if they sank. Then one of the ships in their own squadron, commanded by a French captain thought to be completely mad, fired a broadside into the sinking *Bonhomme Richard.* Jones screamed at him to stop, but the French captain fired again. Desperately, Jones launched a boarding party. Thirty-five men, some of them from the Chesapeake, armed to the teeth and fighting mad, scrambled aboard *Serapis* and began creating havoc. The British abruptly struck their colors.

The battle between *Bonhomme Richard* and *Serapis* would forever be a bright page in American naval history. John Paul Jones became a legend. But those who were there always maintained that without those stubborn, hard-nosed Yankee privateersmen from Forton Prison, the whole thing might have turned out differently.

Source: Durwood T. Stokes, ed., "The Narrative of John Kilby," *Maryland Historical Magazine* 67 (1972): 21–33

▦ 10 ▦

THE MERMAID

In the spring of 1778, after the British army had passed a comfortable winter in Philadelphia while George Washington and his men shivered at Valley Forge, a French fleet left Toulon and broke into the Atlantic, heading for North America. Its commander, Charles-Hector, comte d'Estaing, had been captured by the British in an earlier war, and they knew he wasn't a man to trifle with. Suspecting that d'Estaing intended to help the Americans retake Philadelphia, British general Sir William Howe made plans to leave the city and ordered the navy's frigates to warn His Majesty's shipping away from Delaware Bay, where sooner or later d'Estaing would surely appear.

Among the frigates to receive that order was the handsome little twenty-eight-gun *Mermaid,* under the command of Captain James Hawker, a plump and pleasant-faced young man who had spent the last two years patrolling the American coast. Recently he'd captured a prize and had on board a number of American sailors taken prisoner. Unlike some other British officers, he treated them very well.

On the night of July 6, Hawker and the *Mermaid* were anchored just inside Cape Henlopen, taking on fresh water from HMS *Roebuck,* when they heard cannon fire to the south. It was d'Estaing, announcing his arrival by capturing an American Loyalist privateer just off the Maryland coast. The next morning found the French at the mouth of Delaware Bay. The

Roebuck fled. Hawker remained at anchor, hoping not to be noticed, but the French spotted him. Hawker could now flee north to Philadelphia and be trapped, or try to make the open sea. He chose to run for it.

The *Mermaid* sailed due east, straight at the French fleet until she cleared the "Hen and Chickens" shoal, then Hawker turned south. D'Estaing sent six ships after him. All through a warm, cloudy day, *Mermaid* and her pursuers tacked into a light southwest breeze. *Mermaid* was forced ever closer to shore, until at last she ran aground off Fenwick Island. Fortunately, so did the French. Hawker kept up full sail, and two hours later his boats pulled him off the bar. Three of the French ships managed to get free, too, and soon they were gaining on him.

As he moved slowly down the coast, Hawker threw his drinking water and all but six of his guns overboard, but the game was up, and he knew it. There was only one thing left to do—surrender to the Americans if he could. An American settlement lay just ahead, at Sinepuxent Inlet, where a break in Assateague Island was guarded by American militia. Behind it, on the mainland side of Sinepuxent Bay, was Sinepuxent Towne, a thriving little community the British called a "nest of pirates." Seeing the approaching sails, the Americans ran to their guns and sent several ships into the inlet. James Hawker couldn't have been happier. With the French close behind, he raised his flag for about a minute and quickly lowered it again as he glided into shore. Technically, he had just surrendered to the Americans before the French could get off a shot.

Colonel Samuel Handy of the Worcester County militia took Hawker's surrender. Because he had treated his prisoners so kindly, Governor Thomas Johnson paroled Hawker and his officers and sent them to Philadelphia. Having just put up with a winter-long British occupation, the City of Brotherly Love was somewhat less understanding and revoked the parole, but Congress soon reextended it. Hawker then went to New York, where he was promptly court-martialed for losing his frigate. He was acquitted and went back to England in search of another command.

Down in Sinepuxent Towne, the residents of that so-called nest of "pirates" lived up to their moniker. Saying they took orders only from the State of Maryland, the Worcester County militia fought off all attempts by the young Continental Navy to take the *Mermaid*'s naval stores. Maryland's Admiralty Court rewarded them with about £14,000 worth of stores, and the town rejoiced.

In 1818 a hurricane closed Sinepuxent Inlet, and Sinepuxent Towne drifted away. But today, if you drive across the Verrazano Bridge to Assateague Island and look north half a mile, you can see where a gallant, generous British captain surrendered to a bunch of American "pirates," and no one got hurt.

Source: Roger Novak, "The *Mermaid* of Assateague," *Maryland Historical Magazine* 102 (2007): 194–203

11

MR. SMITH'S BALL

On Christmas Eve, 1803, Jerome Bonaparte, nineteen-year-old brother of Napoleon, married Betsy Patterson, the Belle of Baltimore. Neither the emperor of the French nor the Maryland nobility approved. The couple had fallen in love at first sight, but when he proposed, her parents had refused to give their consent. She had threatened to run away. They had sent her off to relatives in Virginia the night before the wedding. Finally, everyone reached an accord, and the suave, charming French officer married the rebellious young American who thought for herself and argued for women's rights.

Social fireworks were not long in coming. Then, as now, the French took the lead in daring fashions for women, and the fashion that very cold winter ran to gauzy, almost transparent, Empire-style gowns. Naturally, having married into the French ruling class, Betsy was among the first to sport such gowns on this side of the Atlantic.

Her choice of venues could not have been more dramatic. Washington that season was the scene of numerous balls, one week at the Capitol, the next week in Georgetown. Everyone who was anyone attended, including the sharp-eyed and sharp-tongued Rosalie Stier Calvert, who quite naturally commented on what the others were wearing: "The clothes [the women] wear are extremely becoming, [although] some display a little too much—among others, Madame Bonaparte who wears dresses so transparent and tight that you can see her skin through them, no chemise at all. Mrs. Merry, the new English Ambassadress, is very fat and covers only with fine lace two objects which could fill a fourth of a bushel!"

Another socialite, Margaret Bayard Smith, concurred: "I think it no harm to speak the truth. [Madame Bonaparte] has made a great noise here, and mobs of boys have crowded round her splendid equipage to see what I hope will not often be seen in this country, an almost naked woman."

A climax of sorts came when Robert Smith, Thomas Jefferson's secretary of the navy, held a ball at his house in Betsy's honor. "Her appearance was such that it threw all the company into confusion, and no one dared look at her but by stealth," said one shocked guest.

Rosalie Stier Calvert, was also in attendance: "Mrs. Bonaparte came to a dance given by Mr. Smith, wearing a dress so transparent that you could see the color and shape of her thighs, and even more! Several ladies made a point of leaving the room, and one informed the belle that if she did not change her manner of dressing, she would never be asked anywhere again."

The sight of the gloriously gowned Betsy moved Thomas Law, Calvert's nephew and an amateur poet, to write several lines.

I was at Mrs. Smith's last night
And highly gratified my self
Well! What of Madame Bonaparte
Why, she's a little whore at heart
Her lustful looks her wanton air
Her limbs revealed, her bosom bare
. . .
Show her ill suited for the life
Of a Columbians modest wife
Wisely she's chosen her proper line
She's formed for Jerom's concubine.

Law took some of the men aside and regaled them with his poem. That was a mistake, for one of those who heard it was Colonel Aaron Burr, a man who liked to stir things up as routinely as other people stirred their tea. Burr eased himself to Betsy's side and pleasantly informed her that someone had written a very pretty verse paying tribute to her beauty. Naturally, she wanted to hear it and went looking for the poet, who fled to a corner and scribbled a second, more modest and forgettable poem before she found him.

We'll never know precisely what happened to Thomas Law that evening, but the incident added greatly to Betsy's legend and became one more colorful episode in the story she would give the world in the years to come.

Source: Quotes from Margaret Law Callcott, ed., *Mistress of Riversdale: The Plantation Letters of Rosalie Stier Calvert, 1795–1821* (Baltimore: Johns Hopkins University Press, 1991), 77–79

12

THE MOST HATED MAN
IN MARYLAND

These days we like to complain that political campaigns
have become negative, but in the early nineteenth century, Thomas Jefferson's Republicans and Alexander Hamilton's Federalists fought one another with a ferocity we would
never tolerate today.

Newspaper editors were the worst offenders, and no one
outdid Alexander Contee Hanson, who soon became the most
hated man in Baltimore. Hanson was twenty-six and editor of
the *Federal Republican* when the United States declared war
on Great Britain in June of 1812. Federalist to the core, he despised Jefferson and his successor, President James Madison,
whom he felt had led the nation into the wrong conflict. "There
is scarcely an act of tyranny and oppression complained of
against George the Third," he wrote, "which has not been committed by Jefferson and his political pimp...whiffling Jemmy."

A few days after war was declared, a Baltimore mob sacked
Hanson's office and destroyed his press. Hanson escaped to
Georgetown, where he somehow got the ear of Revolutionary
War hero, General "Light Horse Harry" Lee. He then sent an
agent to Baltimore and rented a house at 45 Charles Street.
On July 26, Hanson, "Light Horse Harry," and a few hardcore
Federalists moved in, barricaded the doors and windows, and

smuggled in guns. They also distributed an issue of the *Federal Republican* that had been printed in Georgetown with the Charles Street address on the masthead. A few Federalists in Baltimore joined them, until about thirty men were holed up in the Charles Street house.

Word quickly spread that Hanson was back. At dusk, the first young boys began to curse and throw rocks that shattered the first-floor windows and shutters. More people gathered. Hanson opened a second-floor window and taunted the crowd until it lunged forward and broke down the door. Defenders opened fire. Enraged, those attacking tore open their shirts and cried, "Fire again! Fire again!"

A few doors down the block, at Number 15 Charles Street, General John Stricker, commander of the five-thousand-man state militia, ignored the commotion and ate his supper. Later that night, civic leaders finally prevailed upon him to do something. Stricker ordered William Barney and a squadron of cavalry to quell the riot. At three in the morning, Barney rode down Charles Street just as the mob trundled in a cannon. One fool tried to light it, even though it was pointed at the mob and Barney's men, not Hanson's house. Fortunately, the thing did not go off, but Barney spent the next hour nervously watching the crowd try to figure out how to fire it.

At last Mayor Edward Johnson and General Stricker walked up the street to convince Hanson to surrender. At one point Hanson asked Stricker why he did not call out the Maryland brigade. Stricker pointed at the howling mob across the street and replied, that *was* the Maryland brigade.

Hanson agreed to surrender with his men and be escorted to the jail, which they reached in safety, but then things turned ugly. The mob surrounded the building and tried to push its way in. For some unexplained reason, a deputy opened the door to the cells, and one by one Hanson and his men were dragged outside. One old veteran of the Revolution was killed, another man tarred and feathered. Hanson, "Light Horse Harry" Lee, and the rest were beaten senseless, piled in the street, and left for dead, while tormentors sang, "We'll feather and tar every d————d British tory! And this is the way for American glory."

Hanson survived, and a few years later, when passions had cooled, he told a friend what he had learned about politics. "When I first became enamoured of political pursuits, . . . I considered federalism all that was pure, disinterested and exalted and democracy exactly the reverse," he confessed. "Experience has shown me that the shades of difference between the two parties are but slight, with some few distinguished exceptions among the prominent men on both sides."

Alexander Contee Hanson died in 1819, still the most hated man in Baltimore.

Source: Frank A. Cassell, "The Great Baltimore Riot of 1812," *Maryland Historical Magazine* 70 (1975): 241–59

13

THE SCOURGE OF THE CHESAPEAKE

Born in 1772 to a lowland Scots family with more history than money, George Cockburn joined the Royal Navy when he was ten years old and went to sea at twelve. In 1793, the year revolutionary France declared war on Britain, he turned twenty-one and was promoted to lieutenant. With the Royal Navy's wartime expansion, he was soon given his first command, a small, fourteen-gun sloop named *Speedy*, and assigned to a blockading squadron off the Italian city of Genoa.

The Mediterranean storms were severe that year, and forced the British ships on blockade to run to shelter—except for one. For days no one knew what had happened to *Speedy*, and all feared she was lost, but when the weather cleared and the squadron returned, there she was, never having left her station. Young Cockburn's courage and seamanship greatly impressed the higher-ups and made him a rising star.

Years of war with Napoleonic France followed, with the fearless young Captain Cockburn always in the middle of the action. By 1812, when war broke out with the United States, his was a household name in Britain, and the Admiralty thought he was just the man to bring the war home to the Yankees who had treated British Canadians so roughly. Intending to do exactly that, Rear Admiral Cockburn sailed for the Chesapeake.

He arrived in March 1813 aboard the seventy-four-gun ship of the line *Marlborough* and quickly began creating havoc. Captured coastal shipping was burned or converted to British use as he saw fit. Worse, he strictly applied the harsh law of the sea to Chesapeake farms, plantations, and towns. Cockburn, who also held a colonelcy in the Royal Marines, happily led raiding parties ashore, capturing or destroying military stores, bringing off slaves, and burning houses he deemed to be "hostile." As a British midshipman wrote later, "If by any stretch of argument we could establish the owner of a house . . . to be a militia-man, [then] that house we burnt, because we found arms therein . . . a duck gun, or a rifle. It so happens that in America every man must belong to the militia; and, consequently, every man's house was food for a bonfire."

But that was nothing to what came next. Late in April 1813, Cockburn turned his cold eye on the towns at the head of the bay and began twelve days of terror the likes of which Maryland had never seen.

When Frenchtown on the Elk River dared to fire on his landing boats, Cockburn put it to the torch. On May 3, Havre de Grace met the same fate, and for good measure Cockburn destroyed the important foundry at Principio Furnace. On May 6 he moved up the Sassafras to Frederickstown and Georgetown. When militia ambushed his marines on the river, Cockburn led them ashore with torches blazing.

In a house on the heights above Georgetown, a lone woman, the tall and striking Kitty Knight, whom President Washington had once asked to dance, confronted her unwelcome visitors and defiantly put out the fires as the marines set them. Legend has it that Cockburn himself appeared at her door and that she persuaded him to spare her house and that of her elderly neighbor. The story may be true, but it's just as likely Cockburn was busy supervising the plundering in town, and that it was one of his officers who was so impressed by her courage that they finally left her alone.

On May 7, when Cockburn turned south once more for the mouth of the bay, he left behind almost total destruction. Except for Elkton, where stout defenses had turned him back, the head of the bay was a smoking ruin. When the Admiralty questioned his tactics, Cockburn told them he had burned or taken only military supplies and that he had paid for livestock and other things his crews needed. But his men knew better. One recalled that Cockburn offered five dollars a head for steers worth twenty, a dollar a head for sheep worth six, and, if refused, he simply took what he wanted.

All in all, George Cockburn had done as much as one man could do to destroy part of Maryland. As the *Marlborough* headed south to bring more fire to Norfolk, an angry Virginian offered $1,000 for Cockburn's head, or $500 for each ear. The once gallant young lieutenant had become "the Scourge of the Chesapeake," with a price on his head.

Sources: Christopher T. George, *Terror on the Chesapeake: The War of 1812 on the Bay* (Shippensburg, PA: White Mane Books, 2000); James Pack, *The Man Who Burned the White House: Admiral Sir George Cockburn, 1772–1853* (Emsworth, UK: Kenneth Mason, 1987); Roger Morriss, *Cockburn and the British Navy in Transition: Admiral Sir George Cockburn, 1772–1853* (Columbia: University of South Carolina Press, 1997)

▦ 14 ▦

A FROLIC WITH THE YANKEES

Sometime in the third summer of what would eventually be known as the War of 1812, Captain Sir Peter Parker, twenty-eight years old and said to be the handsomest man in the British navy, accompanied Admiral George Cockburn on a raid that was intended to chastise Americans living near the Chesapeake. Parker was a baronet and the son and grandson of British admirals. He had gone to sea at the age of eight. Cockburn was older, tougher, and without question the most hated man on the bay. Wherever he went, destruction followed. The least suspicion about the sentiments of a household, or the whereabouts of the men in a family, meant that house would be burned to the ground. He now intended to make Parker his protégé in inflicting the harsh lessons of war.

Like any good Royal Navy officer, Parker was a rigid disciplinarian and fearless to the point of being reckless. But in matters less military, his was a slightly gentler sensibility. He'd been educated in the manners and finer tastes of the English aristocracy and was close friends with his first cousin, the poet Lord Byron. Perhaps that is why Cockburn thought it necessary that Parker be tutored in the finer points of making war on civilians.

On this night, Cockburn, Parker, and their raiding party rowed toward a beachside house on the Eastern Shore. Upon entering it, they found three women having tea. As the raiders burst into their parlor, the women shrieked and huddled together.

Cockburn looked around, determined that their husbands and brothers were serving with the Eastern Shore militia, and gave them ten minutes to gather their valuables. The women pleaded. One, a pretty girl of sixteen, dropped to the floor and threw her arms about Parker's knees, begging for mercy. Parker, it is said, looked at Cockburn, his eyes moist. Cockburn merely opened his watch and carefully placed it on the table. When ten minutes had passed, he ushered the women out of the house and ordered his marines to set it afire.

Parker learned the lesson well. When Cockburn left to join Admiral Sir Alexander Cochrane and General Robert Ross on their expedition to capture Washington, Parker remained in the upper bay creating havoc with his powerful frigate, the *Menelaus*. He cruised the Patapsco to within sight of Fort McHenry, then crossed the bay to Kent County and commenced raiding.

Having routed American militia at Bladensburg and burned Washington, Cochrane sailed back to the bay and sent word to Parker to rejoin them. But Parker, unlike his comrades, had not seen any real action. He is supposed to have replied, "I must first have a frolic with the Yankees."

On the sultry night of August 30, 1814, after a fine dinner with his officers and a bit of merry drinking, he and two hundred men lowered away the boats and set off to find a band of militia reportedly camped at Georgetown Crossroads, near Chestertown.

Those militiamen happened to be commanded by Colonel Philip Reed, a tough veteran of the Revolution who had fought under General "Mad Anthony" Wayne. Reed had learned of

Parker's plans and positioned his men in a field of standing corn just where the British would emerge from surrounding woods. Reed primed his guns and quietly waited.

Sometime after midnight, Parker and his sweating men trudged out from beneath the trees into the brilliant moonlight. Suddenly, orange flashes sparkled in the cornfield. Parker ordered a charge, but a bullet severed the artery in his thigh, the same wound that had killed his illustrious grandfather. He lived just long enough to realize that this night would be no frolic.

After a fight of about an hour, Parker's men carried him the five miles back to their boats. Aboard the *Menelaus* his body was placed in a cask of rum for transport to England. At his funeral, in St. Margaret's Church, next to Westminster Abbey, Lord Byron read an especially touching eulogy: "There is a tear for all that die," it began, "A mourner o'er the humblest grave; But nations swell the funeral cry / and Triumph weeps above the brave." And so in England, months after his death, another spoiled young aristocrat was laid to rest amid flowers, gentle tears, and all the trappings of martial glory. Back in Kent County, the men whose houses he'd burned and families he'd terrorized remembered him somewhat differently, as they went about rebuilding their lives.

Source: Benson Lossing, *The Pictorial Field Book of the War of 1812* (1868)

15

THE COOL HAND AND
THE HOTHEAD

In the summer of 1814, Admiral Sir Alexander Cochrane, commanding all British forces on the American station, had with him two remarkable men. The first—Admiral George Cockburn, in charge of British naval forces in the Chesapeake—was irrepressible, colorful, and a terror on the bay. The Americans hated him so much they put a bounty of $1,000 on his head, and $500 on each ear.

The other, General Robert Ross, commanding four thousand British regulars fresh from victory over Napoleon, was Cockburn's polar opposite. A native of Ireland with a bachelor's degree from Trinity College, Dublin, Ross had served with the Duke of Wellington in Spain. Everyone who met Ross admired his quiet confidence and chivalry. Wellington loved him, and so did his men.

So, too, did his wife, Elizabeth. At the end of February 1814, while fighting in France, Ross received a severe wound in his neck. From Bilbao on the north coast of Spain, Elizabeth rode a mule across the Pyrenees to nurse him back to health. When he left for America at the end of June, his wound had not yet healed, and she was distraught.

Ross, Cockburn, and their small force sailed up the Potomac, landed at Benedict, and marched through Upper Marlborough. They had been instructed to be careful, but American resistance was so light Ross began to believe he could actually take Washington. Naturally, Cockburn was all for it. The idea was too risky for Admiral Cochrane, but after twenty-five years in the army, Ross knew an opportunity when he saw it. Ross and Cockburn, the cool hand and the hothead, advanced against orders.

Sure enough, the next day they routed the Americans at Bladensburg, then marched into Washington. Ross sent out a flag of truce to assure the residents they would be safe, but the Americans opened fire from ambush near the capitol, shooting his horse out from under him before being driven off. Ross, Cockburn, and a company of sailors then entered the President's House, ate the meal set for James Madison, and afterward put Washington's public buildings to the torch. Cockburn was simply beside himself. That night, as British officers sat down to dinner in a private home, Cockburn burst in the front door on his mule and doused the candles, saying he preferred to dine by the light of the burning Treasury building across the street.

After a safe return to the ships, Ross couldn't believe his luck. "Our arms have been . . . crowned with a success that I had no reason to expect," he wrote Elizabeth. He told her to keep an eye out for his friend, Captain Harry Smith, who was just leaving for England with the news and would call on her. "This war cannot last long," he wrote. "We then meet . . . *never* again to separate."

The fleet turned north toward Baltimore, and Ross took the army ashore at North Point. When told he was about to meet large numbers of American militia, he said he didn't care if it "rained militia." The next morning, September 12, he ate breakfast with a Maryland farmer. The man asked him if he would be returning for supper. No, Ross said. He would dine that night in Baltimore, or in hell.

With Cockburn at his side, Ross was once more leading his battalions when he ran into another American ambush. This time his horse was spared, but a rifle ball smashed his right arm and entered his chest. An aide gently lowered him to the ground. Ross took a locket from his neck and handed it to Cockburn. "Give that to my dear wife," he told his friend. Just then Cockburn spotted an American rifleman taking aim from behind a tree. He stood up, shook his fist, and roared: "You damned Yankee, I'll give it to you!" Frightened, the man ran off. Gently, they placed Ross on a cart for the journey back to the ships. Later, Cockburn would insist it was that ride that killed him.

On September 27, Harry Smith reached London and brought the joyous news of Washington's burning to the prince regent. He and his wife then traveled to Bath, where they found Elizabeth Ross in high spirits. It would be weeks before any of them learned about North Point and the ambush. By that time, Robert Ross's body had been shipped to Halifax in a hogshead of rum. There he was buried, and there he remains to this day.

Source: Christopher T. George, *Terror on the Chesapeake: The War of 1812 on the Bay* (Shippensburg, PA: White Mane Books, 2000)

16

DEFENDERS

On a hot day at the end of August 1814, as his fleet sailed triumphantly out of the Patuxent and into the bay, British admiral Sir Alexander Cochrane thought about what he would do next. Behind him, smoke still rose from what remained of the President's House and the US Capitol. Aboard his transports, men who had defeated Napoleon in Spain joked about how fast American militia could run.

On the quarterdeck Sir Alexander wondered: What to do about Baltimore? It was, he thought, "the most democratic town and . . . the richest in the union." It had also built the privateers that so far had captured five hundred British ships. Deciding he would either burn it to the ground or impose a devastating ransom, he compared Americans to dogs. "Like Spaniels," he said, "they must be treated with great severity before you even make them tractable."

It was high time though, to be out of the Chesapeake. Yellow fever had scourged the fleet the year before, something Sir Alexander didn't want to repeat, however much that "nest of pirates" beckoned. So he turned south toward the sea, intending to clear the capes, go up the coast, and "surprise Rhode Island" for a month or two until the fever passed. Then he'd be back for a quick visit, before heading for the gulf to take New Orleans and end this war.

In Baltimore, they knew Cochrane was coming for them sooner or later. And they resigned themselves to the fact that he would win. The British were too many, too well armed, too well disciplined, too hardened by experience. They had easily routed American militia at Bladensburg, and now that army was scattered to the winds. What chance did the city have?

But some in Baltimore weren't ready to give up just yet. General Samuel Smith took over the city's defense. John Stricker, head of the Baltimore militia, rallied to his side. They asked Washington for money to pay for their defense, and when the government replied it didn't have much to spare, Baltimore bankers advanced more than $600,000. Individual citizens chipped in more money, as well as loads of hay, beef cattle, and barrels of flour. By the thousands they rose at dawn and dug earthworks on the west side and on Hampstead Hill. From Virginia and Pennsylvania, fresh troops came in to help.

Down at Fort McHenry, the cornerstone of the city's defenses, Major George Armistead drilled his gunners and sent for the huge flag he'd bought the year before. It cost $405.90 and measured thirty by forty-two feet. When the British came, Armistead and his fort would be both visible and ready.

Somewhere near Tangier Island, Sir Alexander changed his mind. No one knows why, but suddenly, frighteningly, the British fleet was beating its way back up the bay. Annapolis panicked as the wave of sail passed, but Cochrane wasn't interested in them.

At 2 a.m. on September 12, his infantry put ashore at North Point, and that afternoon, a few miles up the peninsula, they attacked. Stricker and his militia held them off for two hours until a last furious charge broke the American line. This time, though, the militia didn't scatter. They fell back to the fortifications their neighbors had dug, and regrouped. The next day, Cochrane sent in his bomb ships to destroy Fort McHenry. All through a rain-swept day and night they poured fire and destruction from just beyond the reach of McHenry's guns. Armistead's men could only grit their teeth and bear it. Everyone knew the fort would surely fall. Baltimore's darkest hour had arrived.

Yet the next morning, September 14, Cochrane gave the order to retire. His infantry grumbled, and his frigate captains pleaded for permission to sail in close and blast Fort McHenry to bits. But by now Cochrane had decided it wasn't worth the trouble. Baltimore might not burn this season, but there were other American ports to destroy. Cochrane set a course for New Orleans. As swiftly as they had come, the British sailed away. Behind them the sun broke through the clouds to reveal a stunned, cheering city, an oversized flag unfurling in a freshening breeze, and a Georgetown lawyer inspired to capture this stirring, unbelievable moment in a poem.

Sources: Various, including Christopher T. George, *Terror on the Chesapeake: The War of 1812 on the Bay* (Shippensburg, PA: White Mane Books, 2000)

▦ 17 ▦

THE CHASSEUR

On the night of July 28, 1814, at the height of the War of 1812, a sleek, black-hulled schooner glided undetected through the British blockade outside New York harbor and made for the high seas. She was the *Chasseur*, a fast "clipper" built in Fells Point and commanded by Baltimore's most feared privateer captain—Thomas Boyle.

The thirty-nine-year-old Boyle was known to every admiral, lookout, and gunner in the Royal Navy. As master of the privateer *Comet*, he had wreaked havoc with British shipping in the Caribbean. His first raid alone had brought in $400,000 in prize money. In one sea battle he had gotten the *Comet* in among a small convoy of armed merchant ships and their frigate escort, blasting first one then another for three hours until eventually he took three as prizes.

His plan for the summer of 1814 was even more daring. Knowing the British would be looking for him in the Caribbean, he set a course for the Irish Coast, where convoys from the West Indies broke up, and the ships headed for their home ports. There, where the merchant ships felt safest, Boyle and the *Chasseur* would be waiting.

The plan worked beautifully. On August 16 he captured the *Eclipse,* and three days later the *Commerce.* Two days later he overtook and boarded the *Antelope,* whose captain had refused to fight. Boyle found that shameful and sent his prisoners in to London with a scorching letter to the Admiralty. He then returned to business and in short order captured the *Christiana, Reindeer, Favorite,* and *Prudence.*

Then he did the unimaginable. British admirals off the American Coast—Sir John Borlase Warren and Sir Alexander Cochrane—had declared the United States to be under a state of blockade, even though they hadn't enough ships to enforce it. Boyle thought that was improper. To right matters, he and the hundred or so men of the eighty-five-foot *Chasseur,* cruising off the Irish Coast, now declared the following: "All the ports, harbors, bays, creeks, rivers, inlets, outlets, islands, and sea coasts of the United Kingdom of Great Britain and Ireland" were henceforth "in a state of strict and rigorous blockade." He handed the document to the stunned captain of a ship he'd just captured and told him to take it to the coffee house in London that served as headquarters for Lloyd's maritime insurance. From there he was sure word would spread quickly.

It certainly did. Within days the Royal Navy had every available ship of the line converging on the Irish Sea, intent upon sending the *Chasseur* to the bottom. Boyle turned the little clipper southwest into the Atlantic, but British sails soon appeared everywhere on the horizon. Many the *Chasseur* could outrun. Others she could not. Boyle somehow held them off with his long guns, dodging and running close to the wind. But he didn't exactly flee. Whenever the opportunity arose, he overtook and boarded more merchantmen, declaring them prizes even though the pursuing British soon liberated them again.

The *Chasseur* glided back into New York on October 24, 1814, ending the most spectacular privateer voyage in an age of daring seamanship. Boyle had captured, damaged, or destroyed a million and a half dollars' worth of shipping. British maritime insurance rates went up 33 percent, and a premium was charged anyone crossing the Irish Channel. The Admiralty assigned fourteen sloops of war and three frigates to patrol the Irish Sea. The merchants of Glasgow presented a memorial to the king remarking the "audacity" of American privateers and noting the large numbers of ships captured by a country "whose maritime strength we have hitherto held in contempt."

Back in Baltimore with his wife and six children, Thomas Boyle didn't let success go to his head. The *Chasseur* was in New York, refitting for another voyage, and anyway, Baltimore was still celebrating the victories at North Point and Fort McHenry. As Boyle prepared to go out again, he was probably only dimly aware that in both cities the *Chasseur* was taking on another name. To everyone from Five Points to Fells Point she was now *The Pride of Baltimore*.

Sources: Material from Scott S. Sheads, Fort McHenry National Historic Site; Fred W. Hopkins Jr., *Tom Boyle: Master Privateer* (Cambridge, MD: Tidewater, 1976)

18

THE BATTLE OF THE ICE

MOUND

In the War of 1812, the British navy ruled the seas. They stopped American ships, seized American sailors, burned Washington, lobbed bombs at Fort McHenry, and became a general nuisance. History has recorded their larger accomplishments, but we tend to forget that from 1813 until the end of the war, the Royal Navy made itself completely at home on the Chesapeake Bay, raiding farms and houses on both shores, burning towns, seizing and burning boats, and doing whatever it pleased to make Marylanders miserable.

One such British warship was HMS *Dauntless*, which arrived in the Chesapeake in October 1814. It wasn't much as warships go, just a tender that went around provisioning larger ships. But it had an aggressive young officer aboard, one Matthew Phibbs, who commanded a longboat and a little jollyboat. The longboat contained a cannon and a swivel gun, oars and sails, and twenty sailors and marines, who captured Maryland watercraft and confiscated livestock.

On February 5, 1815, the *Dauntless* anchored off James's Island and the Little Choptank River. The weather was extremely cold. Ice had begun to form on the river, and even in the bay. A peace treaty had been signed in Europe six weeks earlier, but nobody here knew about it yet—news traveled very slowly in 1815. Undaunted by the ice and cold, Phibbs set out the next morning to make mischief.

Imbued with a sense of duty and bristling with a desire to chastise the Americans, Phibbs and his little fleet sailed to the farm of Moses Geoghegan on James's Point, put seven sheep in the jolly boat, and told Geoghegan they'd be back for more the next day. They would have, too, but the next day the jolly couldn't get through the building ice and had to return to the longboat.

Now as it happened, the men of Dorchester County, particularly those who had joined the militia, had had just about enough of the Royal Navy. One of them was Joseph Stewart, a builder of ships that the British had taken. When he heard about Geoghegan's sheep, he gathered a few friends and went down to James's Point to see what was afoot. By then ice coming in from the bay had pinned the longboat against the ice growing out from the shore. Phibbs was stuck. The militia saw this as a golden opportunity but figured they'd need a cannon to capture him, so they went back to Cambridge to find one.

Not Stewart though. The longboat was trapped about four hundred yards offshore, and Stewart noticed that about 150 yards from it the crunching ice had piled up in a sort of mound. He and nineteen other flinty-eyed men loaded their rifles and picked their way across the broken ice, careful not to slip into the freezing water. When they reached the mound, they settled in behind it and opened fire. The British crouched in the longboat and fired back, but they couldn't stand up to work their cannon because the Americans were pretty good shots. After two hours of icy wind and American rifle balls, Phibbs and his men stood up and waved their handkerchiefs in surrender.

Shortly after the shooting stopped, twenty more Shore-men showed up to see what the ruckus was about. Stewart turned his prisoners over to Henry Haskins, deputy marshal for Dorchester County, and the British sailors soon found themselves in the Easton jail. Three weeks later, the peace treaty was ratified.

By May 1815, Phibbs was back in London writing letters to the Admiralty, trying to explain what had happened to his longboat. It was, he said, "captured by the Chesapeake." The Admiralty might have bought that line, but not Stewart, who wrote an account of what he called "The Battle of the Ice Mound" for the *Maryland Gazette*. He also petitioned Congress for compensation. The Committee of Ways and Means referred it to the Committee on Naval Affairs, and eventually Congress awarded Stewart and his men $1,800. Unfortunately for Stewart, all those other Shoremen who'd come by to see what happened got themselves in the bill, too, and when it was all said and done, his share came to $42.90, not much for a victory in wartime. But "the Battle of the Ice Mound" was never forgotten in Dorchester. Stewart got to keep the long-boat, and its cannon became a well-known town monument. One hopes, too, that Moses Geoghegan got his sheep back.

Source: Robert G. Stewart, "The Battle of the Ice Mound, February 7, 1815," *Maryland Historical Magazine* 70 (1975): 372–78

19

JACOB GRUBER

In 1818, as the nation was settling back into the normal rhythms of life following the War of 1812, tension arose between Maryland and its neighbor to the north. Pennsylvania had set in motion the machinery to abolish slavery in 1780. Subsequently, fugitives from the South, many from Maryland, were making their way to freedom in the Keystone State. That angered the Maryland legislature, which demanded that Pennsylvania do something about it.

At just that moment in history, a group of Methodists held a camp meeting outside Hagerstown. Some three thousand people came from miles around to hear the preaching. Most were whites, who sat up front near the speakers. In the rear gathered about four hundred slaves. For some reason or other, the featured speaker failed to appear, and the man who had organized the meeting, a Pennsylvania Methodist minister named Jacob Gruber, stepped up to take his place.

Gruber began by going over the nation's sins—infidelity, drunkenness, profanity—then launched into an attack on hypocrisy. "We Pennsylvanians think it strange," he said, "to read the . . . newspapers, . . . and find '—For sale, a plantation, a house and lot, horses, cows, sheep, and hogs; also, a number of negroes—men, women, and children—some very valuable . . . ; also, a pew in such and such a church.'" This nation holds the

Declaration of Independence "in one hand," he added, "and a bloody whip in the other."

An angry murmur swept through the crowd, and for weeks Hagerstown was in an uproar. At its next meeting, the Hagerstown grand jury indicted Gruber for attempting to incite a slave revolt. A local lawyer took the case and, needing help with Gruber's defense, called upon a bright young friend of his from Frederick, one Roger B. Taney. Taney, who was a member of a local society to protect free blacks and also in the process of freeing his own slaves, got the trial moved to Frederick, a place only slightly more tolerant of abolitionists than Hagerstown.

At the trial, Taney began his defense with a lawyerly argument on behalf of free speech. Under Maryland law, he reminded everyone, no man could be punished for preaching the articles of his religion unless they were immoral or calculated to disturb the peace. Gruber was merely preaching the Methodist doctrine of peaceful abolition. If slaveholders didn't want their slaves to hear that sort of thing, they shouldn't have brought them to the meeting.

As he warmed up, Taney got more direct. "Any man has a right to publish his opinions on [slavery] whenever he pleases," he said. Slavery was a subject of national concern and may at all times be freely discussed. Yes, Mr. Gruber did quote from the Declaration of Independence. "He did rebuke those masters, who, . . . are deaf to the calls of humanity." He did condemn "those reptiles, who live by trading in human flesh, and enrich themselves by tearing the husband from the wife—the infant from the . . . mother," but that was all he had done, and it wasn't a crime.

Taney didn't stop there. Slavery, he said, was "an evil . . . imposed upon us by another nation." It couldn't be "easily, or suddenly removed." And while it remained, it was a "blot on our national character." "Every friend of humanity [should] seek to lighten the galling chain of slavery," he concluded, until the time came when Americans could look upon the Declaration without blushing. One can only wonder what the atmosphere was like in that Frederick courtroom, because the jury deliberated briefly, then returned a verdict of "Not Guilty."

Thirty-nine years later, in the 1857 Supreme Court case of Dred Scott v. Sanford, Chief Justice Roger Brooke Taney would say something entirely different—that a "negro has no rights which a white man is bound to respect." He was referring to what the Constitution and its framers had established in 1789, not his own personal beliefs. But that phrase, taken out of context and widely publicized by Horace Greeley and the *New York Tribune,* would haunt Taney for the rest of his life. Whatever he thought, whatever he had done, he would always be remembered for it.

Unlike Jacob Gruber, whom he had successfully defended on that long ago day in Frederick, Roger Brooke Taney was judged guilty.

Source: Carl Brent Swisher, *Roger B. Taney* (New York: Macmillan, 1936)

▪ 20 ▪

THE BEAR

In the fall of 1834, a man living in what is now Garrett County invited the son of a well-known eastern publisher to visit and go hunting. They found a "paradise" of "grouse, woodcock, squirrels, mountain hare, wild turkey, and deer." But the elk were gone. So were the buffalo that had once roamed the hills. Panthers and bobcats were scarce. And strangest of all, there were no bears. Only thirty years earlier, Western Maryland had teemed with black bears. The visitor didn't know it, but the reason for the bears' disappearance was still prowling the hills.

He was a man just then in his mid-fifties, clad head to toe in buckskin and moccasins, with a rifle over his shoulder and a long knife in his belt. His name was Meshach Browning. He'd been born in Frederick County in 1781, to a poor farmer who died just two weeks after his birth. His mother tried to move the family to Allegany County, but along the way the wagon lost a wheel and went crashing down rocky Sidelong Hill with young Meshach still aboard. Somehow, mangled and stunned, he lived through it. His mother then gave him up to a friendly aunt and uncle who took him out past Cumberland, but the aunt soon turned physically and verbally abusive. To escape her, young Meshach took to the woods. He hunted raccoon and bobcats and traded their fur for a heavier rifle. Farmers paid him a dollar a day to shoot the squirrels that were ravaging their corn.

In 1795 he brought down his first deer. Shortly thereafter he shot a panther said to be eleven feet long. He met a girl, Mary McMullen, three years younger than he was, and killed his first bear, perhaps to impress her. They married and settled on a squatter's farm until the owner chased them off. With an infant daughter, they settled near Bear Creek, a tributary of the Youghiogheny River. The Bear Creek glades were filled with game. All we had to do, Browning said, was "rise . . . slay and eat."

The family made a life in the wilderness that always revolved around the hunt. When the crops failed one summer, Meshach shot panthers and wolves for the bounty. Soon he was staying out weeks at a time, hunting everything, but especially bears.

Bears appealed to him. They were noble and courageous, even when outnumbered. Dogs and bullets wouldn't bring them down. He began picking fights with bears just for the fun of it. Once he freed a bear caught in a wolf trap. "I struck him in the ear as hard as I could, and turned his head round," Meshach said. "He then became mad, and rose on his hind-feet to rake my face or neck, but I struck him in the pit of the stomach which seemed to double him up. . . . He was now in earnest . . . and came again up to the attack." Browning eventually killed the bear with his knife, but people began to doubt his sanity. His wife was sure a bear would kill him one day, and when he jumped from behind a tree to tackle another bear, his brother-in-law, who saw him do it, said he was crazy. Friends implored him to "quit that foolishness" of fighting with a knife after a bear crippled one of his sons, but he only got worse.

He began hunting bears in the winter, crawling into their dens. Once, in the tight quarters of a bear's cave, he fired his rifle and "shuffled out of the hole with my head on fire," he said. He put it out with handfuls of snow.

In 1839, Mary Browning died. The life seemed to go out of Meshach. That fall he killed his last bear, and two years later, his last deer. He was then sixty and beginning to fail, but another reason he left the hunt was the scarcity of game. He had killed most of it himself. By conservative estimates, after thousands of hunts, Meshach Browning alone had killed nearly four hundred bears, more than two thousand deer, fifty panthers and cougars, and scores of wolves and bobcats.

In 1859, as he lay dying of pneumonia in his seventy-ninth year, he overheard one of his sons at his bedside say that the chestnuts were abundant that autumn. A glow came over the old hunter's face. He roused himself and said, "The bears will be there!" But the black bears were gone. It would be 125 years before, under the protection of state laws, they returned to Western Maryland.

Sources: David M. Dean, "Meshach Browning: Bear Hunter of Allegany County, 1781–1859," *Maryland Historical Magazine* 91 (1996): 73–84; *Forty-four years of the Life of a Hunter: Being Reminiscences of Meshach Browning, A Maryland Hunter, roughly written down by himself,* revised and illustrated by E. Stabler (Philadelphia: Lippincott, 1859)

▨ 21 ▨

THE SLAVE BREAKER

In January 1834, a Baltimore man sent a young slave to St. Michaels. The boy, not yet sixteen and named Frederick Bailey, was big for his age and smart. He had enjoyed living in Baltimore, where he had learned to read and had seen many things. But his master feared that his combination of intelligence and literacy might prompt Frederick to run off. So he was sent back to a farm on the Eastern Shore of his birth, to relearn what it meant to be a slave.

For Bailey, St. Michaels was a bad place. His master there could be cruel, but his wife was worse. In addition to beatings, she withheld food as a means of discipline. Young Frederick began to steal food, though he hated himself for doing so. His owner then hired him out to a man named Covey, who ran a nearby farm. Covey was a slave breaker.

Covey sent the inexperienced Bailey into the woods with a cart and a team of oxen. The oxen stampeded into the trees, nearly destroying the cart and knocking Bailey senseless. When he returned to the farm, Covey immediately took him back into the woods. Stopping at a sapling, he cut off a number of switches and ordered the boy to strip. Bailey refused. Covey tore off his clothes and beat him until he bled. Thereafter he beat Bailey at least once a week and reduced his rations.

After six months, the boy was broken. "I was somewhat unmanageable when I first went there," he wrote later, "but a few months of this discipline tamed me. Mr. Covey succeeded in breaking me. I was broken in body, soul, and spirit. . . . My intellect languished, the disposition to read departed, . . . The dark night of slavery closed in upon me."

One hot day that August, Bailey was fanning wheat with three other slaves when he collapsed. Covey appeared and asked what had happened. "Bailey's sick," one told him. Covey walked over to the slumping boy, kicked him, then struck his head with a piece of wood. Covered with blood, Bailey ran into the trees, thinking to tell his master in St. Michaels what the breaker had done.

He stayed the night with another slave at a cabin in the forest. The man strongly advised him to go back, and gave Bailey a root, claiming that as long as he wore it, Covey could not hit him. The next day, Sunday, Bailey returned to Covey's farm. The charm seemed to work, as Covey smiled pleasantly and went off to church.

On Monday morning, Bailey was in the barn grooming the horses when Covey walked in, appearing to have forgotten the whole affair. Bailey was sitting in the loft, his feet dangling over the edge, when Covey grabbed his ankles and tried to tie them with rope. Bailey lunged and landed awkwardly on the stable floor. Covey fell upon him.

"From whence came the spirit I don't know," Bailey wrote later, "I resolved to fight. . . . I seized Covey . . . by the throat; and as I did so, I rose. He held on to me, and I to him." Bailey's fingernails drew blood. Covey frantically called for help. His cousin rushed in and pulled Bailey's hands away, attempting to tie them. The slave dropped this new attacker with a powerful kick and sprang back at Covey. Hands at each other's throats, the two staggered into the barnyard, where two slaves appeared. Covey demanded their help, but both walked away.

At last, exhausted, the slave breaker and the slave released their grips and stood back to take stock of one another. Covey said that that should teach Bailey a lesson.

It did, but not the one Covey intended. "This battle with Mr. Covey was the turning-point in my career as a slave," he wrote. "It . . . revived within me a sense of my own manhood. . . . My long-crushed spirit rose, cowardice departed, bold defiance took its place; . . . The day had passed forever when I could be a slave in fact."

The young slave had become a man. Four years later, Frederick Bailey ran away and joined the antislavery movement. He changed his name to Frederick Douglass, and in fiery speeches he carried across the land the same rage against the evils of slavery that had exploded one hot August day on the floor of a barn near the town of St. Michaels.

Source: William S. McFeeley, *Frederick Douglass* (New York: W. W. Norton, 1991), 44–48

22

MOSES

Sometime in 1836, a young, black Dorchester County slave was hired out to rising shipbuilder and political figure James A. Stewart. She was fourteen, barely five feet tall, and could cut half a cord of wood in a day. Her back, neck, and shoulders were already scarred from beatings, and her forehead bore a terrible scar from a near fatal head injury, inflicted by an overseer, that left her with sleeping spells and dizziness. Stewart put her on a timber gang, work that brought her near the docks and the black watermen who knew the ways of the Underground Railroad. In 1842 their paths diverged. Maybe he knew her name—Araminta Ross—though probably not. Seven years later she escaped to Philadelphia.

More slaves escaped from Maryland than any other southern state, but in 1850 the South toughened its stance. The Fugitive Slave Law permitted bounty hunters to hunt down runaways in the free states, ending any safety they might have found. But Araminta, now Harriet Tubman, had family in Maryland and wasn't about to leave them there.

In 1851 she made the first of several trips back to the Eastern Shore with the intention of rescuing members of her family, especially her sister Rachel. Sometimes she remained on the Shore for months, waiting for the right opportunity and creating havoc for slaveholders.

In March 1857, eight slaves following a route and instructions she had given them made a spectacular escape through Dover. Slave owners reacted predictably. Free blacks were arrested, sometimes tarred and feathered, and told to leave. In May, Tubman managed to bring her parents out, though both were in their seventies. She then returned for Rachel and two of her children before they could be sold to traders from Georgia. In the face of the crackdown, she had to remain hidden, so she gave instructions to others. That October, forty slaves made their break from Dorchester, including one party of twenty-eight, an incredible number. For three days this group slogged through the rain, keeping to the woods and the edges of fields, and once shooting their way through a party of rowdy Irish laborers. But they made it.

Outraged slaveholders gathered in Cambridge and passed resolutions calling for greater protection of their property. One of the most vocal was James A. Stewart, who had been elected to Congress in 1855 and become an outspoken champion of slavery and the South. The "negro," Stewart argued, "is in his happy element on a sugar or cotton plantation, and in this condition will ... scorn the mistaken views of ... Abolitionists to benefit him by placing him on a different theater." The editor of the *Easton Star* boasted that Stewart had "measured lances with, and vanquished, the most powerful champions of abolition."

Perhaps, but Stewart hadn't defeated the tiny, scarred woman who had once been beneath his notice and now was making a public fool out of him right under his nose. Northern newspapers howled with delight as more slaves broke out of Dorchester in December and January.

In the end, the slaveholders won by curtailing the personal liberties of whites and blacks alike. Vigilantes swept through the countryside all but destroying the Underground Railroad in Dorchester, and Harriet Tubman was forced to leave without her sister. Late in 1860 she made one last attempt to rescue Rachel, though by this time slaveholders were watching for her. She reached Rachel's neighborhood only to learn that Rachel had died and that it was impossible to bring out the children. Harriet brought out another couple instead.

It was her last trip as an escaped slave. The next time she came south, it was with a Union army. Harriet Tubman, the woman James A. Stewart never bothered to know, was now called the Moses of her people. And just across the New York border, in St. Catherines, Canada, an entire community of black people who had once been slaves in Dorchester County breathed her name with reverence and joy.

Source: Kate Clifford Larson, *Bound for the Promised Land: Harriet Tubman—Portrait of an American Hero* (New York: One World / Ballantine, 2004)

▦ 23 ▦

GIDU

In the nineteenth-century Maryland colony in Liberia, on the West African coast, the neighboring Grebo people believed in witchcraft. It was an issue important to the colonists.

The freedmen and former slaves who boarded ships in Baltimore between 1834 and 1857 and departed for the West Coast of Africa all dreamed of the different lives they would create for themselves once free in a new land, but one idea they held in common. The new society would be agrarian, Christian, and republican, and it would bring enlightenment to Africa. When they landed at Cape Palmas, they found themselves confronting a people who were in some respects like Englishmen of two centuries before. The Greboes knew how to farm, sail, and handle themselves in trade with outsiders. They were not always kind to the American settlers, and the two groups were frequently at odds, but one African practice stood out as most horrible to the Americans. When something went wrong among the Africans, they cast about for the reason and found it in witches. Unlike the English of two centuries before, those called witches weren't always women. Men were accused, too. The trial to discover whether someone actually was a witch was called "gidu."

It began with sassa-wood, the bark of a tree from the mimosa family, which was peeled off, beaten soft, and soaked in water. The resulting narcotic solution was, if drunk in large quantities, fatal. After someone was accused of practicing witch-craft, he or she was brought to the place of trial, made to sit down, then drink a gallon—or if the offense was severe, two gallons—of the liquid. The poison worked slowly, and the victim was made to walk about for several hours as it reached its full effect. Sometimes it wore off, and the accused was set free. Many times, however, the victim died, slowly and painfully.

Though the Maryland colonists found this custom de-graded and barbaric, there was nothing much they could do about it. In the colony's first months, five villagers from the nearby town of Gbenelu had been forced to drink the poison, and two had died. Then a sixth trial, in October 1834, proved too much for the colony. A Grebo head man named Popo, caught in a political dispute, was to undergo gidu. Popo drank the potion and survived, but his enemies weren't satisfied and arranged for a second trial.

That enraged Dr. James Hall, the colony's agent, who knew Popo as a friend and ally. He attended the second trial and pleaded for the condemned man, but to no avail. "They appeared to owe him a deep grudge, which nothing but his death could appease," Hall said later. The agent had returned to his office and resigned himself to the inevitable, when a Grebo man walked through the door. He told Hall that Popo could indeed be saved if someone of rank and standing took him by the hand as the potion was about to be administered, but Hall should beware. That person would then be responsible for any future misdeeds the accused committed, and might have to take his place.

James Hall was a short, thin, sickly man, who had barely been healthy enough to make the voyage to Africa. After a re-cent accident, he was also hobbling around on crutches. Nevertheless, he rushed to the place of execution on the beach near Gbenelu, falling down a rocky hillside in his hurry.

"I arrived just as they were driving off his wives and children, who had been taking their last farewell," he said. About five hundred people had formed into a hollow square. In the middle, said Hall, "was his Satanic majesty in full panoply, just raising a huge two gallon pot filled to the brim with the poisonous [concoction] to the lips of the wretched Popo." Popo was still reeling from the effects of the previous day's poisoning and was in complete despair. Hall advanced and took hold of his friend, announcing that he would take responsibility for any crimes that could be proven against him. He then led Popo away, "amid the mingled shouts and execrations of his friends and persecutors."

If gidu seems like a strange custom belonging to a time long ago, it isn't. Gidu is still practiced today on the West Coast of Africa.

Source: Richard L. Hall, *On Afric's Shore: A History of Maryland in Liberia, 1834–1857* (Baltimore: Maryland Historical Society, 2003)

▪24▪

THE VINEYARD TOURNAMENT

In August 1839, a Scottish nobleman decided to stage a medieval tournament at his castle in honor of his late countryman, Sir Walter Scott. The great author had died in 1832, leaving much of Britain and the American South infatuated with romantic novels like *Waverly* and *Ivanhoe*.

Lord Eglinton intended nothing like a real tournament, which would have been a ferocious, bloody spectacle. Knights charging one another in what was called the "joust" often meant business. And until Henry II outlawed it, the "joust" was followed by the "grand melee," in which two small armies hacked away with real swords, maces, and battleaxes. All this took place before a mixed crowd, including supposedly refined women, who roared like hockey fans.

Eglinton opted for a much gentler version, one that emphasized costumes, pageantry, and horsemanship. His "knights" would attempt to spear little rings or try to knock down a wooden dummy called a "quintain." When they heard of his plans, dozens of wealthy Americans eagerly took ship for Scotland that summer. Among them was William Gilmor, the son of a prominent Baltimore family.

Like everyone who witnessed the costume opera at Eglinton Castle, Gilmor returned full of romantic notions and decided to stage his own tournament the next year at "The Vineyard," his Baltimore estate near what is now 29th and

Greenmount. He invited a number of wealthy friends from Maryland and Virginia, told them to create medieval costumes, and asked that they come a few days early so they could practice riding at the rings—and the quintain.

Looking back, adding the quintain was probably a mistake. It was a wooden horse with an augur hole bored down through the saddle. A wooden rider was anchored on the horse by weights on chains dropped through the hole. A "knight" who hit it squarely with his lance might knock it over, but hitting it off-center caused it to spin, at which unhappy moment its long wooden arms lashed out to smack the rider in the face or in the back of the head as he rode by. Gilmor might not have known it, but the evil machine's sole purpose on a medieval jousting field was to inflict pain and humiliation. After pitting himself against Gilmor's quintain all day, one guest rode his splendid black charger off the estate and right into the Jones Falls, loudly swearing he'd never get on a horse again.

Somehow though, the tournament came off splendidly. The quintain took its toll, but occasionally the "knights" got it right. Rings were speared. Ladies clapped politely, and the champion offered his crown to his favorite, whom he proclaimed the Queen of Love and Beauty. All hailed Sir Walter Scott, who would have found the whole business a trifle silly. But the South had fallen in love.

After the Vineyard Tournament, jousting spread like wildfire below the Mason-Dixon Line, though the diabolical quintain was quickly discarded. The Civil War put a stop to tournaments, but they returned with a flourish afterward, often as a means to raise money for the southern relief. In 1869 a tournament at Brooklandwood in Baltimore County had carriages backed up all the way to Riderwood.

By then a new and far more cynical day had dawned—the Gilded Age. "The doings of the so-called 'chivalry' of the middle ages were absurd enough, even when they were brutally and bloodily in earnest," Mark Twain snarled in 1870. "But those doings gravely reproduced with tinsel decorations and mock pageantry, by bucolic gentlemen with broomstick lances, and . . . muffin-rings to represent the foe, . . . is absurdity gone crazy." In 1884, instead of selecting his "Queen of Love and Beauty," one champion took his crown and rode off with it. It got worse. By the 1890s, "knights" were riding bicycles, and in 1915 they drove cars, with women trying to spear rings from the passengers' seats.

Today, the best of jousting—the horsemanship, the skill, the good time—survives as Maryland's state sport. But as someone once said, what a long, strange ride it's been.

Source: G. Harrison Orians, "The Origins of the Ring Tournament in the United States," *Maryland Historical Magazine* 36 (1941): 263–77

≡ 25 ≡

THE ROSE OF WESTMINSTER

Baltimore was a booming, brawling town in the 1830s, when, into this rough-and-tumble place, came a sensitive, creative young man. He was about five feet seven, with a broad forehead, curly brown hair, radiant gray eyes, and a tendency to dress like Lord Byron. An acquaintance said his "personal appearance was delicate and effeminate, but never sickly or ghastly, and I never saw him in any dress which was not fashionably neat and with some approximation to elegance."

Born in Boston, schooled in London and at the University of Virginia, he entered the army in 1827 at the age of eighteen. That same year he also published a slim volume of poetry that sold fewer than fifty copies. He enrolled at West Point, but after six months changed his mind, refused to attend classes, and was dismissed. In 1831 he came to Baltimore to live with relatives,

Here he wrote poetry and stories for literary magazines and gathered ideas for future work. A local scandal concerning dentists who got extra teeth by way of professional grave-robbers may have given him the idea for a story entitled "Berenice." The cholera epidemic of 1832 possibly inspired a later piece, "The Masque of the Red Death." In 1833 he became a local celebrity by winning a small literary prize for a story entitled "Manuscript Found in a Bottle."

Still, life was unkind. His older brother died of alcohol or tuberculosis. His books didn't sell. Reviewers were scornful. "Exquisite nonsense," the Boston *Yankee* said of one. The *American Monthly Magazine* said another consisted merely of "some sickly rhymes." The *New York Mirror* described still another as having a "general indefiniteness of ideas" and a "prevailing obscurity."

Dispirited and often depressed, he became devoted to his cousin, Virginia. Though she was not yet in her teens, they shared the same melancholy soul. Once, when out walking, the pair came upon a graveyard where a funeral was in progress and joined the mourners. Though neither of them knew the deceased, both began to weep.

In 1834 his wealthy foster father died, having disinherited him. He moved to Richmond. Unable to bear parting from his beloved cousin, he married Virginia, though she was only thirteen. But life suddenly took on direction. He became the editor of the *Southern Literary Messenger*, moved to Philadelphia, and then New York, where stories began to pour from his pen: *The Narrative of Arthur Gordon Pym*, *Tales of the Grotesque and Arabesque*, *Murders in the Rue Morgue*, *The Gold-Bug*, and, finally, *The Raven*. Although the first printing of *The Raven* brought only fifteen dollars, it made him famous, and it appeared that he had found happiness at last.

But two years and a day after the great poem appeared, Virginia died in his arms of tuberculosis. Mentally and emotionally shattered, he couldn't pull the remnants of his life together. He sought peace in the bottle and courted other women, who dismissed him as a drunk.

To raise money for his own literary magazine, he traveled south once more, arriving in Baltimore on September 28, 1849.

Five days later, during a city election, a compositor for the *Baltimore Sun* found him lying in the street outside Ryan's Fourth Ward Polls, in clothes obviously not his own. The stranger helped him into nearby Gunner's Hall, but the writer was incoherent. They took him to Washington College Hospital, where he lapsed in and out of consciousness until, early on the morning of October 7, 1849, he died. One who was at his bedside said that his last words were, "Lord, help my poor soul." He was buried in the Westminster Burying Ground in Baltimore, leaving behind him a never-to-be-forgotten body of work, and a nation's literature given new shape and energy.

To this day, each year on January 19, his birthday, a kindly, remembering soul leaves a bottle of brandy and a rose in Westminster, at the grave of Edgar Allan Poe.

Source: Various biographies of Poe

■ 26 ■

CHRISTIANA

In September 1851, Edward Gorsuch, a farmer in northern Baltimore County, decided to go up into Pennsylvania and bring back four slaves who had run off two years before. Gorsuch, who was considered to be a good Methodist and mild slave master, had told his slaves he'd free them when they reached the age of twenty-eight, and he couldn't understand why these men in their mid-twenties had run off. He was determined to persuade them to return. Right was right, and after all, they were his "property."

One had fled farther north, but three had taken refuge near the small town of Christiana, close by Lancaster. Acting under the Fugitive Slave Law, passed in 1850, a small posse of policemen from Philadelphia was already moving on Christiana to support Gorsuch.

Lancaster County was home to thousands of African Americans. Many had fled slavery in Maryland and Virginia, and they had been fighting slave catchers for years. Leading them against slavers and the gangs of white working-class thugs who roamed the countryside was William Parker. Now twenty-nine, tall, lean, and muscular, he had met Frederick Douglass when they were both slaves in Maryland. Like Douglass, Parker knew how to fight. But unlike Douglass, he made fighting his business. When he and his men caught up with slave catchers, they beat them within an inch of their lives, sometimes beyond.

At dawn on September 11, Gorsuch, his party, and the Philadelphia policemen surrounded a small, isolated, house where the runaways were said to be hiding. As Gorsuch and the marshal approached the doorway, into it stepped William Parker himself. "If you take another step," Parker warned, "I'll break your neck."

"I have heard many a negro talk as big as you," the marshal replied, "and then have taken him; and I'll take you."

"You have not taken me yet," Parker said. From upstairs came the sound of men loading rifles.

As Gorsuch tried to persuade his three slaves to return, Parker's wife leaned out an upstairs window and blew a horn to signal neighbors that something was wrong. The posse fired ten or twelve shots, trying to silence her, and she ducked inside as bullets clacked against the fieldstone. From another window, someone sent a bullet past Gorsuch's ear.

The posse withdrew to talk things over. Gorsuch's son, Dickinson, advised them to leave for now. Half an hour passed, and the marshal shouted that he was ready to burn down the house. It was too late. Nearly a hundred blacks, and a few whites, armed with rifles and farm tools, were walking toward them across the rolling fields from every direction.

Fearing a battle, two of the former slaves surrendered. Dickinson pleaded with his father to be satisfied and return home, but old Edward would not leave without all of his "property." He walked back into the yard and confronted the last man, Samuel Thompson, who suddenly clubbed his former master with a large pistol, then shot him as he fell. Other blacks shot him, too. Then one emptied a shotgun into Dickinson Gorsuch, who staggered off with a terrible wound in his side. The posse fled, pursued by angry, jeering men. An elderly black man threw himself across young Dickinson and stopped the mob from tearing him to pieces.

Edward's body was sent home. Dickinson recovered in a nearby farmhouse. William Parker led the former slaves north to Rochester, New York, where his old friend Douglass sped them across the border to a new life in Canada. Gangs of deputized thugs, some released from the penitentiary for the emergency, swept through Lancaster County, roughing up and arresting anyone suspected of helping the fugitives. In January, a grand jury convened but found no reason to indict anyone— all the principals were dead, gone, or in Canada.

As fear cast its long shadow across Pennsylvania and Maryland, people recalled what William Parker had said to a white neighbor who had come to plead with him not to fight. "The laws for personal protection are not made for us," he'd told her, "and we are not bound to obey them. . . . the whites . . . have a country and may obey the laws. But we have no country."

Source: Thomas P. Slaughter, *Bloody Dawn: The Christiana Riot and Racial Violence in the Antebellum North* (New York: Oxford University Press, 1991)

27

JOHN BROWN

On the morning of Friday, December 2, 1859, two thousand soldiers, officials, and townspeople gathered around a gallows in a field on the outskirts of Charlestown, Virginia. Just before eleven, a wagon bearing the condemned man approached. Tall and spare, wearing a long white beard, and with his arms tightly bound at the elbows, he was sitting on a black walnut coffin and had to be helped to the ground. But when he climbed the scaffold, his step was lively. Like some Old Testament prophet, he stood in the sun and gazed through the "warm and dreamy haze," at the fields and mountains beyond. "This *is* a beautiful country," he said. The sheriff removed his hat, placed the rope around his neck, and drew a white hood over his head.

Then, a full ten minutes passed while soldiers and officials sought their assigned places.

The old man remained steadfast and calm. Some in the crowd murmured at the courage of one they so hated. For this was John Brown, the notorious abolitionist, feared and hated by every southerner. Three years earlier, he and his sons had hacked five proslavery men to death one windy spring night in "Bleeding Kansas." From there he had come east, to carry on his personal war against the South. With promises of support from prominent men in Massachusetts, he had drawn up a constitution for the republic of ex-slaves he would form in the

Appalachian Mountains. He wanted no bloody uprising, he said, only a place where slaves could find protection, and he would begin by seizing weapons from the federal arsenal at Harpers Ferry.

In July he registered at a Hagerstown hotel under the name of Isaac Smith, a cattle buyer from New York, and waited for his sons and supporters to arrive. As they trickled in, he hid them in the attic of a farmhouse he'd rented outside Sharpsburg, seven miles from the ferry. Two of his daughters arrived to cook and do the laundry. As months passed while Brown waited for the weapons he'd been promised, nerves grew taut. Neighbors became suspicious. One barefoot and nosy old woman even entered the house when the daughters were away and confronted one of his men. Brown knew he had to move. He also changed his mind. This would not be the start of a peaceful revolution at all. Now he was going to cross the Potomac with fire and sword.

On the moonless night of October 16, he led eighteen raiders through a light drizzle, down the twisting mountain path into Harpers Ferry. Quickly and silently they took the armory and its supply of rifles. With a handful of raiders and several hostages, Brown then took shelter in the engine house and waited for word to reach the slaves, certain that they would flock to him.

What came instead were scores of armed, angry townsmen and farmers who drank heavily in the hotel and shot down Brown's men as they found them, two under a flag of truce. Colonel Robert E. Lee arrived at the head of some US Marines, who battered in the engine house door, killed Brown's sons, and nearly killed Brown himself.

After a short trial in Charlestown, he was sentenced to hang. As he awaited the fateful day, he wrote eloquent letters to his supporters. The last, handed to a jailer as he left for the gallows, delivered a chilling warning: "I, John Brown am now quite certain that the crimes of this guilty, land: will never be purged away; but with Blood."

At last the sheriff got things straightened out, and with one blow of his axe cut the rope that sprang the trap, launching John Brown into the next world. Across the North, those who hated slavery rang church bells and gathered to honor a fallen hero, a martyr to a just and rightful cause. Across the South people rejoiced too—they now had their vengeance.

In the crowd, a talented young actor from Bel Air smiled approvingly as the body was lowered into its coffin. Like Brown, who sought martyrdom, he also longed for fame and recognition. He would find it, too, a little more than five years later, near the end of the terrible bloodshed that John Brown had predicted would befall the nation. But unlike Brown, who would be celebrated in song and story, the name of John Wilkes Booth would forever reside in the darker chapters of American history.

Source: Stephen B. Oates, *To Purge This Land with Blood* (New York: Harper and Row, 1970)

⬛ 28 ⬛

APRIL 19, 1861

In 1907, an aging Union army veteran sat down to write about his Civil War. Ernest Wardwell was fourteen and a student at "the Adams School" in Baltimore when the Confederates fired on Fort Sumter, and when the first columns in Federal blue marched into his city on their way to Washington.

"The nineteenth day of April 1861 . . . dawned clear and bright. . . . Newsboys were shouting 'all about the Yankee invaders' who were coming to pillage our city. Groups of men and even women stood on the street corners, . . . Everybody seemed full of patriotic fire, . . . Knots of men . . . carrying guns and pistols hurried through the streets. . . . Suddenly the fire-bells began to ring, and . . . the principal said that we were dismissed."

Ernest and his pal, Henry Cook, raced to the President Street railroad station. All around them, men swore the Yankees would never make it into town. Then the train carrying troops from Massachusetts and Pennsylvania arrived in a cloud of steam and smoke. Drivers hitched teams of horses to the cars for the journey up President Street to Pratt Street and across the waterfront to Camden Station, where the B&O train to Washington waited.

The boys could plainly see the Massachusetts men as the mob angrily hurled bricks and stones at the car windows. Teamsters cracked their whips and drove straight into the gathering mob, which closed around them "like an army of howling wolves."

Shouts and curses drew Ernest and Henry back toward the station, where another group of Yankees were setting out on foot. As they turned onto narrow, crowded Pratt Street, Baltimore men darted at the neat ranks, trying to seize a rifle. From the upper stories people threw "great lumps of coal, stone jars, bottles, pitchers, dishes, . . . every conceivable form of weapon." Men in blue staggered; a few fell.

At Marsh Market the crowd was so thick the troops could not move. An officer climbed a pile of stones and shouted, "Men of Baltimore, we have no quarrel with you. We only ask the right of transit through your city to obey our orders." Before he could say more, someone heaved a heavy piece of wood that struck him on the head. His men shielded him with their bodies.

That sight changed Wardwell's life. "I felt the officer's appeal was right, these soldiers were not to blame, they were but obeying orders. . . . I began to feel . . . sympathy for them, . . . their bleeding faces and hands awoke pity; . . . Their gallant bearing, showing no fear of the angry mob, or attempt to use their weapons, aroused my admiration."

Ernest pushed his way through to a Yankee sergeant and offered to carry the rifle of a man who'd fallen. "Go way, or I'll run it through you," the sergeant barked over the crowd noise. Ernest said he was only trying to help. "*Are* you?" said the sergeant. "Well then, fall in."

Guns now flashed in the windows. More soldiers fell. At Gay Street, the lead company fired over the mob's heads, trying to frighten them back, but the "wolves" only grew bolder. "They won't shoot. They're too afraid of their cowardly necks!"

Reluctantly, the wounded officer told his men to fire. The mob was so close the soldiers could barely aim their rifles, but they obeyed. "My brain was in a whirl," Wardwell recalled. "I saw dozens of men lying on the street and curbs, as we ran by, and I heard the shrieks and groans of many more." A soldier running beside him said, "Don't be scared, we will soon join the rest of the regiment and then it will be all right." Ernest clung to his arm.

When they reached the safety of Camden Station, Ernest hesitated, then got on the train. The friendly soldier, whose name was Parsons, gave him a seat by the window, pulled off the boy's old black slouch hat, and replaced it with a blue soldier's cap. "He also gave me a drink out of his canteen. It tasted very good indeed, being rum and molasses." Dazed and excited, the boy sat back in his seat as the train pulled out of Camden Station. Young Ernest Wardwell was off to war.

That night he and his new comrades—the Sixth Massachusetts Regiment of Volunteer Militia—would sleep on the floor of the House of Representatives. It was a lot for a boy not yet sixteen to comprehend, and it was too soon to know that he would never see his friend, Henry Cook, again.

Source: Frank Towers, ed., "Military Waif: A Sidelight on the Baltimore Riot of 19 April 1861," *Maryland Historical Magazine* 89 (1994): 427–46

29

CLARA'S BOYS

On the afternoon of April 19, 1861, a train filled with Union volunteers rattled its way south to Washington. They were Massachusetts men, who had just been mobbed on Baltimore's Pratt Street. Many were cut and bruised from hand-to-hand fighting with the crowd. A few carried bullet wounds.

News of the riot had flashed across the telegraph wires, and in Washington, hundreds rushed to the railroad station. Among them was a small, dark-haired woman of thirty-nine who worked in the patent office. Formerly, she had been a schoolteacher in Worcester, and as the regiment passed, she recognized many in the ranks. They had been her students—her boys. Secessionists in the crowd jeered and mocked. The schoolteacher became "indignant, excited, [and] alarmed," and vowed to do something.

Washington had no military hospital or barracks. The wounded spent several days in makeshift quarters throughout the city, including the Senate chamber itself. The former schoolteacher and her sister took some of the seriously wounded home with them. The soldiers' baggage had been left in Baltimore. They had no rations. Many had "nothing," she said, "but their heavy woolen clothes—not a cotton shirt and many of them not even a pocket handkerchief."

The next morning the women persuaded neighborhood grocers to sell them as many provisions as they could and delivered the food and drink to their boys. They emptied their closets and bureaus of "combs, thread, needles, . . . pens, buttons, strings, salves, [and] tallow," and gave them out. They tore up old sheets for towels and handkerchiefs, packed wicker baskets, and went to the capitol building. The schoolteacher sat in the vice president's chair and read aloud to her homesick and confused boys from a copy of their local paper, joking that it was "better attention than I have been accustomed to see . . . in the old time."

In the next days and weeks, more troops arrived, until an army surrounded the city. Caught up in the patriotic excitement, the women went to the camps every day, handing out homemade cake and jam. "I don't know how long it has been since my ear has been free from the roll of a drum," the schoolteacher wrote her father, "it is the music I sleep by and I love it." Soldiers, too, wrote letters home, telling friends and family what the sisters had done for them. In response came hundreds of packages from mothers, wives, and daughters, until, their rooms packed to overflowing, the two women moved to larger quarters.

The excitement built to a climax in July, when the untested Union army marched into Virginia to meet a similar army of boys eager for battle—these from the newly formed Confederate States of America. A number of Washingtonians went, too, packing picnic lunches for an exciting afternoon at a place called Bull Run. The sisters remained behind. First reports were encouraging, but by the end of the day the boys were coming back, frightened, bitter, and bloody. This time the wounded pouring in from the battlefield numbered in the thousands. "A sad, painful, and mortifying scene," wrote the schoolteacher, for whom the day became a turning point.

Henceforth, she took the skills she'd mastered nursing sick relatives, teaching rambunctious boys, and organizing free county schools in Massachusetts, New York, and New Jersey, and channeled them into providing aid for the wounded and comfort for those stricken by the shock of war. "So far as our poor efforts can reach," she pledged, "they shall never lack a kindly hand or a sister's sympathy."

Years later, many a Washingtonian would remember the tiny dark-haired woman, perched atop a large, unsteady wagonload of goods, holding on as best she could, "while crowds of well-dressed people walked sedately to church." Clara Barton, angel of the battlefield and founder of the American Red Cross, had discovered her calling in those first frantic days after the Pratt Street riot, when she nursed the men—her boys—who had shed the first blood of the American Civil War.

Source: Elizabeth Brown Pryor, *Clara Barton: Professional Angel* (Philadelphia: University of Pennsylvania Press, 1988)

30

LOST SONS

In the spring of 1862, George Alfred Townsend was twenty-one years old and very much pleased at his situation. A major New York newspaper had just offered him a job covering what looked like the end of the great war between the states. Townsend, who had no intention of joining the army, nevertheless longed for adventure, and this assignment could launch his career. At six in the morning he boarded a train in New York, passed through his native Philadelphia at eleven, and arrived in Baltimore at three. By five he was aboard a steamboat gliding down the Patapsco River toward Fortress Monroe, Virginia, and the great Union army advancing on Richmond.

The trip down the bay took fourteen hours, and three or four hundred people were aboard the steamer. A quarter of them were army officers and a few wives. About half were contractors and other civilians who saw in the war the key to making their fortunes.

That night, as Townsend stood alone at the rail watching the sunset, a lone woman approached him. She was pale. Her face was thin, as though she had been hungry for a long time, and her clothing was threadbare. She told him she was from Baltimore and asked if he knew the surgeon-general at Fortress Monroe. Townsend replied that he did not. "The fact is," she said softly, "I am going to Williamsburg to—find—the—

body—of my—boy." She shivered, and covered her eyes with a thin, white hand.

Townsend assured her that anyone in Federal service would be glad to help her, but she looked up at him and said, "He was not a Federal soldier, sir. He was a Confederate!" She insisted it wasn't her fault. The boy had been living in Richmond when the war broke out. Now she was afraid that when she found his body they wouldn't let her take him back home to Baltimore, which was under Union army control. "He was my oldest boy," she said, "and his brother, my second son, was killed at Ball's Bluff; *He* was in the Federal service. I hardly think they will refuse me the poor favor of laying them in the same grave."

Townsend explained that it wouldn't be easy to find her son's body. His grave was probably unmarked.

It was "a sad thing," she said, "to know that one's children died enemies." His name was James. Both brothers had been at the battle of Ball's Bluff, on opposite sides. What if James, the Confederate, fired the shot that killed his little brother, William?

The supper bell rang, and a crowd of soldiers, sutlers, and contractors stampeded into the dining salon. Townsend offered to find the woman a seat at the table, but she refused. To save what little money she had, she had brought a small amount of food and planned to spend the night on a chair in the salon. She bid him good-bye and walked away.

Townsend went in to dinner, where men "rushed to the tables like as many beasts of prey." An army captain made short work of a whole mackerel, then grabbed the plate of butter and spread the entire half-pound on a single slice of bread. A sutler reached across Townsend's face and speared a chicken with his fork, then, to everyone's disgust, wolfed down the whole thing himself. A waiter approached with a plate of steak. Before he could set it down, two soldiers seized it for themselves. "Eat all you can," laughed one. "The fare's amazin' high. Must make it out in grub."

There was a piano in the salon, and a few women joined the men in singing "The Star-Spangled Banner." A soldier got out his hornpipe, and several couples began to dance. One young man bellowed out a passage from Shakespeare.

"The night passed by gleefully and reputably," Townsend recalled later. But the young correspondent couldn't forget the pale woman from Baltimore. "One could hardly realize, in the cheerful eyes and active figures of the dance, the sad uncertainties of the time," he wrote of that night. He did not know then, as he would soon come to know, that he had seen two faces of this terrible war. One was masculine—heedless of danger, driven variously by passion, glory, patriotism, sacrifice, corruption, and greed. The other moved quietly in the shadows, as lonely women in numbers Townsend could not yet fathom, moved sadly and slowly across the war-torn landscape, often cold and hungry and alone, searching for loved ones who would never return.

Source: George Alfred Townsend, *Rustics in Rebellion: A Yankee Reporter on the Road to Richmond, 1861–1865,* with an introduction by Lida Mayo (Chapel Hill: University of North Carolina Press, 1950)

31

BARBARA FRIETSCHIE

Barbara Hauer was not the sort of woman the people of Frederick could easily ignore. Born in Lancaster, Pennsylvania, in 1766 to parents who had survived a tough voyage from the German Palatinate, she was nine when the Revolution broke out and fourteen when a neighbor was hanged in the public square for being a loyalist.

Barbara was a patriot, who, it was said, had entertained George Washington himself. She was also independent. Only at forty did she finally marry, and then she chose John Frietschie, fourteen years younger and son of the hanged loyalist neighbor. When John died in 1849, Barbara lived on in her house at the edge of town as a dignified widow of keen mind and sharp tongue. She attended the Evangelical Reformed Church every Sunday and doubtless showed the flag on the Fourth of July.

So her life progressed until the summer of 1862, when beautiful, staid, prosperous Frederick was suddenly turned on its head. On September 6 and 7, thousands of dusty, foul-smelling Confederate infantry suddenly filled the streets and shops. And the Rebels, fresh from their victory at Second Bull Run, were not shy about telling Union citizens what they thought of them.

Their commander, the redoubtable Stonewall Jackson, came into town Sunday evening, fell asleep in church, and left the next morning, taking his regiments with him. As the gray columns tramped west out Patrick Street, heading toward South Mountain and Harpers Ferry, several officers tied Union flags to their horses' tails and dragged them through the dust. Suddenly, an old woman rushed out of her house, shook her long, bony hands at them, and cursed them for degrading the flag. Some thought it was Barbara Frietschie.

A few days later the Army of the Potomac thundered into Frederick, and Barbara waved her flag at the boys in blue as they followed the rebels west to Sharpsburg. A few days later, Frederick's churches and schools overflowed with wounded. For months, the great battle at Antietam was all the people of Frederick could talk about. They were still talking about it in December when, at the age of ninety-seven, Barbara Frietschie died.

A year passed. Stories grew. Washington novelist Emma Southworth wrote a letter to her friend, John Greenleaf Whittier, relating a tale of heroism in Frederick just before the battle. The *Atlantic Monthly* paid Whittier fifty dollars that October for a poem entitled "Barbara Frietchie." It was an account of those mad days in September of 1862, in which Stonewall Jackson, at the head of his men, spotted an old woman waving a Union flag from her attic and ordered his men to shoot it down. In reply she delivered a withering blast of her own: " 'Shoot, if you must this old gray head, / but spare your country's flag,' she said."

Southerners were apoplectic. Northerners flocked to Frederick to see that attic window and pester Barbara's neighbors with questions. Jacob Englebrecht, who lived just across Patrick Street, exploded in frustration. The poem "*is not true*," he insisted. "For three days I was . . . looking at the Rebel Army passing the door . . . and should anything like that have occurred I am certain some one in our family would have noticed it."

Barbara's house was torn down in 1869, but the controversy raged on. Did she actually do it? No one really knew. Union and Confederate generals were called upon as witnesses. Mrs. Thomas J. "Stonewall" Jackson herself waded in to assure everyone her husband would never shoot a lady. But in 1892, another novelist, Caroline Wells Dall, said she'd found evidence that Barbara had been Whittier's defiant heroine, and the story took on new life. In 1926, Barbara's house was rebuilt as a museum. In 1943, Winston Churchill stood in front of it and recited Whittier's poem. Dwight D. Eisenhower and Theodore McKeldin dropped by in 1952.

The legend of Barbara Frietschie was proving to be as durable and determined as old Barbara Hauer herself.

Source: Dorothy M. and William R. Quynn, "Barbara Frietschie," *Maryland Historical Magazine* 37 (1942): 227–54

32

THE DESPOT'S HEEL

During the Civil War, Union troops occupied a number of forts around Baltimore, including one on Federal Hill. We've come to think rather badly of these "Yankees," who posed for photographs leaning against giant cannons aimed directly at the city's heart. They were the ruthless tyrants, the "despot's heel" of James Ryder Randall's wartime anthem, "My Maryland," still the state song. But who were they, really?

In December of 1862, they were mostly farm boys from upstate New York who had enlisted out of patriotism and a need for the bounty money offered by their towns and counties. They were not mercenaries. They had just come through years of bad crops, and most took the bounty to save their farms.

Baltimore didn't exactly dazzle them, but they generally liked it. The more daring ran the guard so they could spend a night on the town, flirt with local girls, drink in saloons, and taste their first oysters. They relished army food mainly because there was enough of it. "I gained [two] pounds last week and I way a hundred and sixty one pounds and a half and I think that is doing pretty well for me," one told his sister. "Em it is most diner time and I must close for I would not loos my diner for nothing for it would make a lean streak mother always said."

They waited eagerly for packages from home, and were overjoyed when they arrived. "I et some of Mother Fullers good cake and cheese [and] some of Mrs Cookes good Preserves and cake, Butter &c," Jasper Dean told his family. "If you send some dried Fruit I can stew them here. I dont think it would be best to send aney apels yet," he added, but "send two or three just for a taste."

Lieutenant Marshall Cook, who was better off than most, joked how the honey his brother Irving had sent leaked onto the coat and blanket in his package, then invited Irving to take the train down to visit him. First they went to Mt. Vernon Square and spent thirteen cents each to climb the 200 steps of the Washington Monument. "After going up a winding stair case inside of the shaft we found ourselves at its summit," Irving told his wife. The statue high above their heads, which on the ground had looked, he said, like "a mere toy," now looked like "great coarse monsters which forcibly reminded me of the saying of the Poet—or someone else that 'distance lends enchantment to the view.'"

The pair climbed down and next found their way to the "Union Relief Association," marveling how it fed two thousand men at a time. "Its astonishing to see the amount of food disposed of there each day," Irving reported. "The . . . cheese alone amounts to . . . 10 to 12 hundred pounds daily—besides thousands of pounds of beef—and piles of bread." One of the head men told them that two or three hundred Baltimore families, who had lost husbands or brothers in the war, survived on the crumbs.

The New Yorkers pretty much knew how that felt, for they had lived close to it. They always thought first of their own families. When they were finally paid, two brothers and a cousin pooled their money and sent $165 home, keeping only $1.65 each for themselves.

On Christmas day, 1862, they took part in Baltimore's festivities. "I just came in from down town," Jasper Dean gushed to his mother. "This Regt has all been peradeing through the streets makeing a big show. The Baltimoreans are selebrating Christmas . . . the same as we do the forth of July."

As they got ready for the Christmas meal, another soldier sat down to write his mother. Before enlisting, Jack Eaton, nineteen years old, from Genesee County, had tried to support his sister, little brother, and their widowed mother on the money he made as a farm laborer. His mother had just sent him a pair of woolen gloves she'd knitted herself, to keep him warm on guard duty against the raw Baltimore cold. Now, he told her, he had sold them for two dollars, and he was mailing the money home to her. "They was most too costly for me to wear," he said. "Make good use of it."

It turns out that there was more to the "despot's heel" than we ever knew, and probably more to the Civil War than we'll ever know.

Source: Kathryn Lerch, "The Eighth New York Heavy Artillery," unpublished manuscript

33

THE GLORIOUS FOURTH . . .
1863

From the 1780s into the nineteenth century, the Fourth of July was the premier American holiday. Bands played, militia drilled, politicians gave overlong speeches, and fireworks crackled and boomed into the night. Baltimore laid the cornerstone for the Washington Monument on July 4, 1815. Thirteen years later, Charles Carroll of Carrollton, last living signer of the Declaration of Independence, laid another cornerstone, this one for the B&O Railroad.

But the holiday's luster had begun to fade. In 1826 the *Frederick-Town Herald* stopped publishing dinner toasts on the grounds that they were "generally dull, insipid affairs, about which few feel any interest." President Zachary Taylor ate too many fresh cherries and drank too much iced milk all at once while celebrating in 1850, and fell mortally ill. In 1853, hundreds of rowdy Baltimoreans on an excursion to Annapolis got into a fight with the locals that left two dead.

Then came the War of the Rebellion and the terrible summer of 1863, when it began to look like a nation celebrated might soon become a nation only dimly remembered. The great Rebel general, Robert E. Lee, brought his dusty columns north, spoiling for a fight that would end the war. Terror spread across Maryland and Pennsylvania as the Rebels fanned out, looking for ransom and supplies. On Wednesday, July 1, the Army of the Potomac caught up with them at Gettysburg. All day Wednesday and into Thursday, the armies gathered their strength and sized up one another, but all anyone in Baltimore knew was that some of their sons, brothers, and husbands were in for it—men in the Confederate First Maryland Battalion, the Third Maryland US Infantry, the Potomac Home Brigade and the First Eastern Shore Regiment, Rigby's Battery, Brown's Chesapeake Artillery, the First Maryland Cavalry.

By Friday, July 3, city papers were reporting Wednesday's news. That day Baltimoreans also read a directive from General Robert C. Schenck, military commander in Baltimore, prescribing how the Fourth of July would be celebrated. No one was to leave the city. "Let every man on that day show his colors" by flying the American flag from his house, Schenck ordered: "If there be any spot where it does not appear, its absence there will only prove that patriot hearts do not beat beneath that roof." Within hours, large stores and small shops alike beheld a run on American flags.

About one o'clock that Friday afternoon, those rushing to buy flags stopped what they were doing and listened as a heavy and ominous sound, like the rumbling of a summer storm, swept across the city.

Fifty-eight miles away, on Seminary Ridge, a hundred Confederate guns had opened fire, and on Cemetery Ridge, ninety Federal cannon roared in reply. The resulting thunder, lasting an hour and a half, was clearly audible in Baltimore.

The next day, the Fourth of July went on much as Schenck had planned. Baltimoreans would not learn about Little Round Top, the Wheatfield, or Pickett's Charge for several more days.

The city had no idea, as it celebrated the "grand and glorious Fourth," what had taken place at Gettysburg or that the armies now glared at one another across a once peaceful landscape covered with thousands of dead and dying men and horses, a sight so powerful that some of those who saw it would later go mad. But in Baltimore there were brilliant displays of fireworks to enjoy at the intersection of Broadway and Baltimore Street; at Monument, Madison, and Union Squares; and on Federal Hill. Schenck had also lifted the order against leaving the city— at least as far as Druid Hill Park, so that loyal citizens could "visit that popular and pleasant resort." American flags, if not everywhere, were abundant.

That night, back in Gettysburg, as the Confederate troops were quietly trying to make their escape from the great battle, someone threw handfuls of firecrackers among the ambulances groaning with wounded. The noise stampeded the horses and spread panic among the troops.

So ended the Fourth of July, 1863.

Source: Baltimore Sun, July 3–7, 1863; James R. Heintze, http://gurukul
.american.edu/heintze/fourth.htm#Beginning

🕮 34 🕮

THE ORATOR

In the summer and fall of 1863, the once pretty town of Gettysburg, Pennsylvania, just across the Mason-Dixon line, was a grim and horrible place. After the great battle in July, both armies had left their dead where they had fallen. Soldiers and local residents, pressed into the job, covered eight thousand bodies in shallow graves. But relatives, rushing to the battlefield in search of lost loved ones, dug up the bodies and rifled their pockets for identification, then moved on. Housewives stepped around corpses in their vegetable gardens. Farmers wondered how they would plow their fields. A young Gettysburg banker named David Wills sent an urgent wire to Pennsylvania governor Andrew Curtin, asking for help.

Facing a difficult reelection campaign, Curtin wanted the problem solved, so he made Wills his agent. The young banker created an interstate commission to raise funds. A contractor agreed to rebury the dead for $1.59 per body. Wills found someone to design a new cemetery, and he laid plans for its dedication in October. To highlight the ceremony, he invited the nation's premier orator, Harvard president Edward Everett.

Everett was the star in a golden age of oratory, in which audiences stood through speeches of two or three hours, hanging onto every word, every gesture. Everett had crafted speeches for Daniel Webster and dedicated battlefields at Lexington, Concord, and Bunker Hill. He would be honored to speak, he told Wills, but he couldn't meet the October deadline. There was much research to do first, and however long the talk, he always spoke from memory. He had to rehearse. Wills set a new date—November 19.

When Wills learned that at least ten thousand people from all over the North were coming, he thought that a few remarks by President Lincoln might also be in order. A few weeks before the ceremony, he extended the invitation to the White House. The short notice was not unusual. This was, after all, a state function in Pennsylvania, not a national one, and Lincoln was not offended. But the master politician was eager to come. He had his own campaign to think about, and he wanted his aides to circulate among the dignitaries and political leaders in the crowd, and gather intelligence.

Thursday, November 19, dawned a splendid day, with a clear sky and some late fall color lingering in the trees. The procession left town on schedule and arrived at the cemetery by noon. From a raised speakers' platform, the Reverend T. H. Stockton read a prayer. Above and behind him, onlookers could see the graves, perhaps a third of them recently filled, many freshly dug. Beside the platform, the flap of a tent opened, and Edward Everett emerged with a thick sheaf of papers—his oration—which he ostentatiously placed on a small table beside him. He wouldn't touch it again. For the next two hours, he was all that anyone could ask for in a speaker. He recalled how the ancient Greeks honored their dead after the battle of Marathon, and compared the invading Confederates to the Asiatic hordes of Persia, bent on bringing slavery to the land. He pointed to the now well-known places on the field—Round Top, the Devil's Den, the Wheatfield and Peach Orchard, Seminary Ridge, Cemetery Ridge—and described each phase of the battle. He picked up the doctrines of secession and states' rights, broke them in his hands, and hurled them down. "As we bid farewell to the dust of these martyr-heroes," he concluded, "in the glorious annals of our common country, there will be no brighter page than that which relates The Battles of Gettysburg." The audience applauded. They had heard a masterpiece. A hymn began.

Then Abraham Lincoln rose to his feet. In a high tenor voice that carried his Kentucky accent to the far reaches of a crowd estimated now at almost twenty thousand, he began an address of only 272 words: "Fourscore and seven years ago, our fathers brought forth upon this continent a new nation, conceived in Liberty, and dedicated to the proposition that all men are created equal."

The rest is history, a history in which Edward Everett would be all but forgotten.

Source: Garry Wills, *Lincoln at Gettysburg: The Words that Remade America* (New York: Simon and Schuster, 1992)

35

COLOR GUARD

They were called a regiment of slaves. In the summer of 1863, after the Battle of Gettysburg, Robert C. Schenck, the military commander of Baltimore, informed President Abraham Lincoln that the city had at least two thousand free black men who were willing to fight for the Union. White volunteering had dropped off. Colonel William G. Birney was ordered to begin recruiting black troops.

Birney was the son of a wealthy New England abolitionist and had no intention of limiting his regiment to the free black clerks, mechanics, shipbuilders, and craftsmen of Baltimore City. To fill his ranks, he put a well-drilled squad and a few musicians on a small steamer and cruised up and down the bay. Wherever he put in to shore, the squad drilled, the band played, and slaves made their way to the boat. When his steamer hit Dorchester County, home of Harriet Tubman, ninety-three slaves enlisted. Birney found more recruits in the slave pens of Baltimore, where Washington area planters had sent their property for protection. The first thousand men were commissioned the Fourth US Colored Infantry.

They joined up for any number of reasons. "I will fight as long as a star can be seen and if [it] be my lot to be cut down in battle, I do believe . . . that my soul will be forever at rest," said one. Another, who had been "bound out" in Harford County since childhood confessed, "I thought that the war would be something like gardening. . . . I found it . . . to be . . . very different from that."

In 1864 the regiment joined the Army of the James, under the flamboyant, and incompetent, General Benjamin F. Butler. They first saw action that summer as Union forces closed in on Richmond and Petersburg. Disease and minié balls thinned their ranks. Soon the regiment numbered only four hundred men.

By then the war in the East had become a series of desperate battles for the Confederate capital. On September 29, the Fourth found itself spearheading an attack on a place called New Market Heights. They would make a bayonet charge across a swamp and a steep ravine, cut their way through two rows of sharpened stakes, and storm a bluff defended by artillery and riflemen from Texas and Arkansas.

"When the charge was started, our Color guard was full; two sergeants (carrying the Colors) and ten corporals," said Baltimore clerk Christian Fleetwood. But, he added, those Rebels "knew how to shoot." Men fell as they crossed the marsh and ravine and threw themselves at the stakes. With hatchets they worked frantically to cut an opening. Then a bullet shattered the regimental flagstaff and killed the bearer. The charge stalled. Alfred B. Hilton, a farmer from Harford County, six feet tall and carrying the national flag, grabbed the falling regimental colors and carried both flags forward until a bullet shattered his leg. Fleetwood and Baltimore fireman Charles Veal seized the colors and charged on. A handful of men made it to the top, only to be blasted to bits. Those who realized they were alone and tried to surrender were shot down. The Rebels were not taking black troops prisoner.

The regiment retreated, leaving half its number killed or wounded. Fleetwood wrapped the colors around his body to protect them. A second black regiment charged the bluffs and was driven back, but a third charge, rushing through the openings the others had created, broke through and captured the heights.

In the larger scope of things, the battle for New Market Heights was not important except as an incidence of remarkable courage. Of the Fourth US Colored Infantry's original twelve-man color guard that day, only Alfred Hilton, returned alive, and he later died of wounds. Hilton, Charles Veal, and Christian Fleetwood were all awarded the Medal of Honor. Think of them, the next time you see a color guard, and remember, too, the gallantry of Maryland's "regiment of slaves."

Source: Edward G. Longacre, *A Regiment of Slaves: The 4th United States Colored Infantry, 1863–1866* (Mechanicsburg, PA: Stackpole Books, 2003)

36

THE MUSIC OF POINT

LOOKOUT

In November 1864 a steamer approached the landing at Point
Lookout, the prison camp Union military authorities had
established at the southern tip of Maryland, at the point where
the Potomac meets the Chesapeake Bay. A group of Confederate prisoners were prodded onto the dock and made to stand
in the biting November wind while guards inspected them and
kicked into the bay anything with a "US" stamped on it—especially blankets and warm overcoats. After a time, when the prisoners were sufficiently miserable with cold, they were marched
into the compound, or "bull pen," and assigned to tents.

Union policy was to keep them alive, but just barely. Rations
were meager. On Christmas day the year before, when President
Lincoln himself had visited the camp, one prisoner wrote his
family: "It was cold and clear and I was . . . cold and hungry all
day," he said. "Only got a piece of bread and a cup of coffee for
breakfast and a small slice of meat and a cup of soup and five
crackers for dinner and supper I had none." The men slowly
starved. When a long-dead seagull washed ashore, one man
ate it on the spot.

Firewood was also kept deliberately scarce—"about a cord
of green pine to one thousand men for five days," one prisoner
said, "It was mockery." "I noticed a pale-faced soldier lying op-

posite me," said another, "his old shoes were sockless, and his tattered pantaloons reached to a few inches below his knees, leaving a bare and naked space. I . . . reached over . . . and took hold of his leg, which was just as cold as an icicle, and he did not awake. . . . he had become so hardened to cold."

Among the prisoners arriving on that steamer in November was a young Georgian named Sidney Lanier. He was more poet and musician than soldier, and on the dock, before the guards inspected him, he slipped a prized possession, his flute, up his tattered sleeve. Once inside the camp, freezing and fighting off hunger, he began to play.

The sound reached the ears of a man on the other side of the "bull pen." His first thought was that "it was an angel imprisoned with us to cheer and console us." Years later he remembered the sight of the young Georgian standing in the twilight, playing that flute. "The night sky, clear as a dewdrop above us, the waters of the Chesapeake far to the east, the long gray beach and the distant pines, seemed all to have found an interpreter in him. In all those dreary months of imprisonment, . . . his was the clear-hearted, hopeful voice that sang."

Lanier managed to get out of Point Lookout with the help of a friend who bribed a guard, but it was too late—he had contracted tuberculosis. He returned to Georgia, and after the war came to Baltimore to teach poetry at the new Johns Hopkins University. One of his colleagues was John Tabb, his tentmate from Point Lookout, and a man so bitter he vowed never to cross the Mason-Dixon Line. Both played in the Peabody Orchestra until, in 1881, Lanier died.

Haunted by the tune he had first heard at Point Lookout, Tabb reproduced it for a friend, who arranged it into a piece called "The Melody from Lanier's Flute." The music made its way first to the Peabody Orchestra, then to the Boston Symphony, and finally to the White House itself, where it was played by the United States Marine Corps band.

Source: Robert I. Cottom Jr. and Mary Ellen Hayward, *Maryland in the Civil War: A House Divided* (Baltimore: Maryland Historical Society, 1994), 104–7

37

HETTY CARY

In the heady days of May 1861, as the drums beat for civil war, Baltimore became a hotly divided city. Union troops marched in, planted cannon on Federal Hill, and replaced civil authorities with the military.

Among those who openly defied the army's orders not to show support for the new Confederacy was a group of young women known as the "Monument Street Girls," after their neighborhood around the Washington Monument. One of them—Hetty Cary—stood out. Witty and strong-willed, she was still unmarried at twenty-five, though her auburn hair, dancing eyes, and perfect figure prompted many a young blade to declare her the most beautiful woman in the South. One day, as a Union regiment marched down Eutaw Street past her house, Hetty leaned out her second-floor window and waved a Confederate flag over their heads. When the troops angrily called for her arrest, their colonel replied, "She's beautiful enough to do as she damn well pleases!"

As time went by, though, Hetty was warned to leave Baltimore. One night in July, with her brother and sister, she crossed the Potomac and was taken by friends to Richmond, where she soon moved in the highest social circles.

In September, on the invitation of General P. G. T. Beauregard, the Cary sisters inspected the Maryland troops and sang for them a poem, written by a young New Orleans schoolteacher, called "Maryland, My Maryland," that the Monument Street Girls had set to the tune of "O, Tannenbaum." That autumn, a congressional committee asked the Cary sisters to sew the first new Confederate battle flags, the "Southern Cross" that we know today.

In the spring of 1862, Hetty fell in love. His name was John Pegram, and he was a dashing officer—well bred, darkly handsome, and brave—but militarily incompetent. In western Virginia, he had ignored his pickets' warnings that they were about to be surrounded, and shortly thereafter had the distinction of becoming the first West Point graduate to be captured in the war. While on parole and awaiting exchange in Richmond, he met Hetty at a party and determined to marry her.

Then, as now, war was not kind to lovers. The army sent him west to Tennessee, while the Cary sisters remained in Richmond, socializing and dining at Robert E. Lee's table in the Spotswood Hotel. But Pegram persisted. Transferred east, he caught a bullet in the leg at the Wilderness. He recovered, and on January 19, 1865, all of Richmond society converged on St. Paul's Episcopal Church to see their wedding. The omens weren't good. A mirror broke while Hetty was putting on her gown. The horses pulling her carriage to St. Paul's reared and became uncontrollable. And finally, on entering the church, she dropped her handkerchief, and when she stooped to pick it up, her veil tore in two.

Nevertheless, the ceremony went on, while cannons boomed in the distance. Their honeymoon cottage would be a farmhouse near Petersburg—his headquarters.

Eighteen days later, a Union sharpshooter spotted Pegram, who was now a general, and took careful aim. He didn't miss. As Pegram's men brought his body back to the farmhouse, they passed an ambulance where Hetty was making bandages. "I heard her laughing," a captain said later, "while she sat there waiting for him." No one had the heart to tell her what had happened, and she passed the night in their bedroom, unaware that her husband had been laid out in the room just below. When informed of the terrible news the next day, she rushed downstairs and tenderly removed a locket containing her picture, and the watch she had wound for him just twenty-four hours earlier. Both were stained with blood. Three weeks to the day after their wedding, Hetty Cary knelt beside John Pegram's coffin in St. Paul's, as the minister who had married them performed the funeral service.

Hetty returned to Baltimore. Only in 1879 did she remarry, this time to a Johns Hopkins physiologist. Thirteen years later, at the age of fifty-six, the most beautiful woman in the South, who had sung the first rendition of "Maryland, My Maryland" and sewn the first Confederate battle flags, died, closing a poignant and little-known chapter of "Your Maryland."

Source: With thanks to Prof. Cary Woodward, for supplying materials for this piece

⬛ 38 ⬛

THE GREAT PATAPSCO FLOOD
OF 1868

At 5:45 on the morning of July 24, 1868, an express train left Mt. Airy for Baltimore. For weeks it had been 100 degrees or hotter, with little rain, but after the train had gone about two miles it came under a terrible storm cloud. The sky grew black. Suddenly, there was a deluge. "It did not rain," said one passenger, "it poured . . . as if a lake had fallen, in mass, upon us." Thunder broke all around. "Red and blue streaks" of lightning split trees and telegraph poles. As it rounded a bend well above the Patapsco River, the train plowed into a mudslide, embedding itself. "This proved our salvation," said the passenger, "for the flood could not sweep us off."

For hours, unable to move, sixty people endured what they had never seen before. Rainwater came down the vales to the river so fast that it shot out over the edge of the cliffs, "dashed through the tops of the . . . pine trees," then struck the opposite shore. Three-inch hail shattered the cars' glass windows. It sounded, witnesses said, "like nothing else but the noise of battle." Soon, "houses, barns, hay stacks, logs and cattle" careened by.

Downstream in Ellicott City, the sky grew so dark that shopkeepers lit lamps and millworkers stepped away from their looms, unable to see in the fading light. Some walked up the nearby hills, an action that probably saved their lives. One man noticed the rising water and set off to warn the mills but was turned back by the sudden tide.

In the next half hour, the river rose twenty-five feet. The water hit the first dams, formed a wall that rolled back on itself sending spray twenty feet high, then broke through.

Dr. Thomas B. Owings lived with his wife, six children, and a family of African American servants in a new three-story frame house in the center of a row of thirteen built on a kind of island near the Patapsco Flour Mill. Against his wife's wishes, he had responded to an urgent call to see a patient that morning and was on his way back when the flood struck the Granite Factory just upstream, shattering walls that were twenty feet thick at the base.

As the flood tore at the first of the houses upstream from his home, Thomas Owings climbed atop a stone house on the hillside and called to his wife to get the children to the top floor. A neighbor boy climbed onto the rooftops and scurried across the Owings' roof, jumped into the rushing water, caught hold of a rope, and pulled himself onto the Patapsco Mill bridge. The Gabriel family climbed into the Owings house when their own crashed against it, shoving both across a twelve-foot alley.

Inside the Owings house, the head of the African American family—William, no last name recorded—seized an axe, ran up to the garret, and began chopping a hole in the roof. One by one he pulled Margaretta Owings, her children, the Gabriels, and his own family up and outside. Other neighbors cut their way into the Owings garret and climbed out until between sixteen and nineteen people desperately clung to the Owings' roof. When it collapsed, they climbed to the next roof, then the next.

From the bank, Thomas Owings and others called to them to keep moving, keep moving, but the water relentlessly tore at the foundations, collapsing one house after another, until the refugees huddled on the last one. Then, it broke and swept them all away in the murderous, churning river. Men seized Thomas Owings to keep him from diving after his family.

Thirty-six people in the little row of houses were lost that day. In the aftermath of the tragedy, the community looked for heroism. "Everybody is speaking of the bravery and devotion of Dr. Owings' man William," wrote one newspaper. Another picked up the story. But soon, a different man, a white foreman, was given credit for chopping that hole in the roof and pulling the families out. It was a more socially appropriate ending, especially in those first years after the Civil War, when racial antagonism in Maryland was acute. William disappeared from history. To this day, no one knows his last name.

Source: Henry K. Sharp, *The Patapsco Valley: Cradle of the Industrial Revolution in Maryland* (Baltimore: Maryland Historical Society, 2001)

39

GHOSTS OF WESTERN
MARYLAND

The mountains of western Maryland are a scenic wonder, a source of pride, and a great place to live or visit. They're also where people have seen a number of ghosts. For example, sometime before the Revolution, an Indian chief with the odd name of Twenty Bones was buried near Linesboro with his musket, copper beads, and pots of food. Locals thought the grave was cursed, but a drifter who heard the story in a tavern thought that was nonsense. One night someone saw him go out with a pick and shovel. When he didn't return, the townspeople went out to look for him, and naturally they started with the chief's burial mound. It had been opened, but the chief was still there. So were his musket and copper beads. But the pots of food were open, too, and from the pots, droplets of what looked like blood formed a trail that led into the forest. No one ever saw that drifter again.

The old Westminster jail had a ghost, that of Big Tom Parkes, a giant of a man from Tennessee. When he was arrested in 1846 for blasphemy or striking a woman, no one knows which, it took two deputies to bring Big Tom in, with the sheriff holding a pistol against his head. Tom drew a long sentence, and rather than serve it, he committed suicide with his own knife on Christmas night.

The town coroner happened to be William Zollickhoffer, the famous author of a medical textbook then in wide use and a member of the Union Mills Scientific, Literary, and Philosophical Society. Phrenology was all the rage in 1846, and Zollickhoffer got permission to remove Big Tom's head so he could examine its bumps for clues to the criminal personality. No one knows what he found, but for years afterward, the ghost of poor Tom Parkes spent nights roaming the jail—pathetically holding his arms out before him, as though looking for his missing head.

As you might expect, the Civil War greatly increased the ghost population. A pastor in Burkittsville reported hearing the sound of tramping feet on warm nights in late summer and seeing ghostly campfires in the distant meadows. Critics said the fires were only marsh gas and fireflies, but others thought they might be warming the soldiers who died at the Battle of South Mountain in September 1862.

A nearby tannery that had served as a field hospital after the battle for Crampton's Gap had to be abandoned in the early twentieth century. A young couple thought it was a nice, quiet place to park, until the next morning, when they found human footprints on the hood and roof of the car. They hadn't seen or heard anything at the tannery—but the footprints wouldn't wash off. Someone suggested it might be the wounded soldiers who had died there, wanting recognition. When the local American Legion Post stepped in and dedicated a monument to them, the footprints stopped.

After the battle at Fox's Gap, a number of Confederate dead were dumped down the well of the Wise farm, and a little dirt was thrown over them. One night before going to bed, old man Wise was standing in his doorway when a dark figure beckoned to him from the well. Trembling, Wise asked what it wanted. The specter replied, "I'm Jim Tubbs, and I'm buried in a damn uncomfortable position. Turn me over, will you?" The next day, Wise opened the well and turned over the topmost body. That was the last time they saw Jim Tubbs.

Long after the war, residents and Appalachian hikers reported smelling gunpowder and hearing the clash of sabers in the night. Smoke appeared where there was no fire and coalesced into long lines of pale figures.

Near Washington Monument, a Union soldier had deserted just before the fight at Antietam and gone to live with his girlfriend in Zittlestown. A year later, he and the girl both disappeared. The people of Zittlestown figured the men he had deserted had come back, killed them both, and buried them near the monument. For years, each September, those living or camping near the monument claimed they could hear the sounds of battle in the night. They also heard the girl cry and moan. And in the morning, the grass around the monument was always trampled flat.

These stories and many more can be found in a delightful little book, *Tales of Mountain Maryland*, by Paula M. Strain. Read it, and the next time you visit the mountains, you'll know what it is you hear, or see, in the dark.

Source: Paula M. Strain, *Tales of Western Maryland, with a Special Section on the C&O Canal* (New York: iUniverse, 2005)

◼ 40 ◼

EARLY RACING AT PIMLICO

Legend has it that one day in 1868, Maryland governor Oden Bowie got so carried away at New York's Saratoga race track that he proposed a new stakes race to be held in Maryland. New York merchant Milton H. Sanford, who had made his money selling blankets to the Union army, put up $15,000 for the prize in the new "Dinner Party Stakes." Bowie guaranteed the prize and the race. The trouble was, Bowie didn't have a track. Baltimore horsemen raced at the Huntingdon Avenue fair grounds or up and down Charles Street Avenue.

There was one other place, owned by an eccentric Englishman who had grown up near Olde Ben Pimlico's tavern in London. Transplanted to northwest Baltimore, he had plowed a circle on his estate and called it a track. In December 1869 the place fell into the hands of the Maryland Jockey Club. The next fall, Pimlico, as they called it, became Maryland's answer to big-time racing.

On October 26, 1870, Bowie's Dinner Party Stakes finally came off. To the surprise of many and the disgust of those backing the favorite, the winner was a colt named Preakness, whom aficionados described as a cart horse. In fact he was a thoroughbred, sired by the famed Lexington and owned by none other than Milton Sanford of the Civil War blankets.

Preakness ran the two miles in three minutes, forty-seven and a half seconds. A street was named for his jockey, William

Hayward, and a new race was named after the horse—the Preakness Stakes.

The 1870s became the first golden age of Maryland racing. With its ornate Victorian clubhouse and handsome spires, Pimlico was every bit the equal of tracks in New York, Louisiana, and Kentucky. In 1876, tobacco magnate Pierre Lorillard, inventor of the tuxedo and owner of a stud farm in New Jersey, won the Preakness with his colt Shirley. Lorillard would figure prominently in what came to be known as "the great sweepstakes at Baltimore."

On October 24, 1877, three horses came to Pimlico for a race intended to match the best in the country. From Kentucky came Ten Broeck, winner of eight out of eight starts in the West. Representing the East was 1875 Preakness winner Big Tom Ochiltree. And from New Jersey came Pierre Lorillard and a colt with the unlikely name of Parole, of whom, it was said, "no great deeds were expected." Hotels quickly filled up as race fans flocked to the city. Congress adjourned and took the train for Baltimore. The Kentuckians drove the odds, betting heavily on Ten Broeck. Lorillard took every bet. No one was betting on Parole.

On race day, at twenty minutes past three, before a crowd of twenty thousand, the horses approached the starting line. Ten Broeck broke first, with Big Tom on his flank and Parole a length behind. At the three-quarter pole, Ten Broeck led by half a length, and at the one-mile mark, Parole was four lengths behind. Big Tom's jockey gave him his head. The two favorites went neck and neck, but the trailing Parole began to gain ground. The second time the horses passed the three-quarter pole, Parole flew by Big Tom and caught up with Ten Broeck. As they rounded the last turn Parole moved in front and a hush fell over the crowd. They galloped into the final stretch looking, one reporter said, "like a string of three with the wrong end coming on." Parole finished three lengths ahead of Ten Broeck and six ahead of Tom Ochiltree.

The crowd mobbed Parole's jockey and nearly tore off his colors. Hundreds of Kentuckians went bankrupt, and Lorillard made another fortune. The Maryland Jockey Club profited handsomely and used the money to build a spur line from the Western Maryland railroad to the race grounds. Soon it was possible to take the train from City Hall to Pimlico for a round-trip fare of fifty cents—an amount within the workingman's reach. Maryland racing was off and running.

Source: Laura Rice, *Maryland History in Prints, 1743–1900* (Baltimore: Maryland Historical Society, 2002)

⁙ 41 ⁙

PREAKNESS

In 1831, on receiving word that his father had died, eighteen-year-old Milton H. Sanford left Captain Partridge's Military School and rushed home to Weymouth, Massachusetts, to take over the family's cotton mills. Despite a severe economic depression six years later, he built a textile empire. During the Civil War, his fortunes got even better, when he moved to New York and won government contracts to make blankets for the army. Soon Milton Sanford was a *very* rich man, and like a great many wealthy men, he turned his attention to the sport of kings.

He bought some land in northern New Jersey, near the city of Paterson, which had opened a racetrack in 1864 with the Jersey Derby, the first derby to be held in the United States. Local Indians had named the land, its creek, and nearby forest *Pra-qua-les*, meaning "quail woods." English settlers in the 1690s shortened that to "Prake-ness," and by the time Sanford bought it, the place was called "Preakness." Sanford brought a British trainer and jockey named Billy Hayward to his Preakness Farms to train thoroughbreds, and it was here that he also brought an oversized, dark bay colt that he'd picked up at auction in Kentucky for $4,000. Sanford named him after his farm.

The next year, following a lovely late summer day of racing at Saratoga Springs, Milton Sanford threw a grand dinner party at the Union Hall Hotel. When someone proposed that an annual stakes race be held for three-year-olds, Maryland governor Oden Bowie, a great horseman himself, offered a $15,000 purse and promised to build the track for it at Pimlico, on the outskirts of Baltimore. They decided to name the race after the evening's festivities, and in October 1870, Sanford brought Billy Hayward and three-year-old Preakness down to Baltimore to race in the inaugural "Dinner Party Stakes."

There were some that day who sneered at the big bay's size and wondered why Sanford was entering a "cart horse" in a thoroughbred race. But the laughter quickly faded as Preakness powered to the lead and won by a length, and smiling jockey Billy Hayward untied the purse containing Oden Bowie's prize money from a wire stretched above the finish line. In 1873 the Maryland Jockey Club opened Pimlico's first spring meet with a stakes race named for Preakness, who had gone on to win more than his share of races. Two years later, Sanford shipped the horse to Great Britain and, after he won the Brighton Cup, put him up for auction.

Here the story takes a darker turn, for the man who bought Preakness was none other than William Douglas-Hamilton, the Twelfth Duke of Hamilton and a headstrong ne'er-do-well. His ancestor James, the first Duke of Hamilton, was a loyal but incompetent commander of Scottish forces defending Charles I. On being captured, he'd been beheaded, and by the mid-nineteenth century, the family's fortunes had sunk even lower.

William Douglas-Hamilton's father had moved to Paris with his wife because she resented not being made first among the other duchesses. After a night of competitive drinking at the Maison Doreé, he had stepped outside, fallen down, gone home, and promptly died. That left the family's Scottish castles and a magnificent house in London to William, who squandered the fortune and avoided bankruptcy only by betting heavily on a national sweepstakes winner.

William was thickset, crude, and something of a lout. As a student at Oxford he'd taken to boxing and appeared "strong enough to fell an ox with his fist." He evidently treated animals with the same tenderness, for it wasn't long before Preakness became difficult to handle. One night, after what was vaguely described as "an incident in the stables," the hot-tempered duke shot Preakness and killed him.

When it became known that a great horse had died at the hand of a spoiled aristocrat acting on a whim, the resulting uproar rattled all of British society. Parliament responded with reform laws to define and prevent cruelty to animals, especially horses. So as we celebrate the Preakness, here in Maryland where it belongs, we should remember the colt who started it all, and the lasting good he brought about in a life that ended far too soon.

Source: www.lambertcastle.org/preakness_race.html

▨ 42 ▨

THE GREAT RAILROAD STRIKE
OF 1877, PART I

Friday, July 20, 1877, was a cool, clear day in Baltimore after two weeks of suffocating heat. Workers ended the week with a trip to the saloons to talk about the depression that had begun wrecking their lives four years earlier and showed no signs of ending. There was also exciting news—the railroad men had struck the B&O.

In 1877 railroads were the equivalent of today's energy or software companies, frighteningly wealthy and wielding tremendous power. Men like Franklin Gowen of the Reading, Thomas Scott of the Pennsylvania, and John Work Garrett of the B&O bought governors and entire legislatures when necessary.

To keep profits up, they were cutting expenses. Crews were forced to maintain homes at both ends of the line and received no pay while they waited between trains. Acting in concert, railroads up and down the East Coast cut salaries by 25 to 50 percent over four years and beat down all opposition. When engineers on the Boston and Maine struck for an extra ten cents a day, a sum that would have cost the road $47 a week, the company broke them.

Everyone knew that railroading was dangerous work. Brakemen, running across the tops of cars in sleet and snow to turn the brake wheels and handle unhooded couplings had the worst of it. The saying went that a brakeman with both his hands and all ten fingers was incredibly skillful, impossibly lucky, or new on the job. For this dangerous work, they received $1.75 per twelve-hour day. Some never came home. Tired, desperate, and discouraged, they sometimes let themselves fall between the cars.

When a railroad man was injured or killed, his family asked the railroad for assistance. The response often led to court proceedings. "The case . . . has resulted in a verdict of $2,500 for the plaintiff," B&O counsel John H. B. Latrobe informed Garrett after one of many trials. "The jury were probably influenced by the consideration that . . . $45 was a small sum to compensate for the injuries the man had received, including a rupture that would endure for life."

Just days before that cool Friday in July, some strange news had come out of Martinsburg. A couple of B&O crews had brought their trains in, run the locomotives into the roundhouse, and refused to go out again. Soon more crews got involved. At Garrett's insistence, Governor Henry Mathews called out the militia, and gunfire soon echoed in the West Virginia hills. Also at Garrett's request, President Rutherford B. Hayes sent in troops, including the hard-bitten Second US Artillery out of Fort McHenry.

The trains were no sooner running out of Martinsburg than new incidents erupted in Wheeling, Keyser, and Grafton. Men who had taken trains through those mountains came back with a need for whiskey and told tales that could hush a barroom—twilight ambushes, chilling howls and curses in the woods, pistol flashes in the darkness.

In Baltimore, working people wanted the government to stay out of it. "Let them fight it out," they said, of management and the strikers. They resented corporations for making their lives miserable, and they especially resented men like Garrett.

Even Garrett's friends began to doubt the wisdom of rewarding stockholders at the expense of his employees. One wrote, "The sympathies of so many are with the *poor* strikers. Can't you condone their error . . . it is all the power they have—and help them? Let the stockholders and those more able to lose be the ones, and not these poor working men. It is for bread they strike." Then he got personal. "You cannot, in the ease and plenty in which you live understand their pressing need—for wife and little ones. How far will the small pittance they get go towards the support of a family? Oh, be magnanimous . . . and do something."

But it was too late. When the train carrying the federal troops back from Martinsburg stopped in front of the Queen City Hotel in Cumberland, a mob surrounded it. Hordes of young boys scampered between the cars, uncoupling them and locking the brakes. The troops fingered their rifles, but held their fire.

Clearly the great railroad strike had not died in Martinsburg. It was rolling toward Baltimore.

Sources: Robert V. Bruce, *1877: Year of Violence* (Indianapolis: Bobbs-Merrill, 1959). For quotes, see letters to Jonathan King of the B&O Railroad, manuscript collection at the Maryland Historical Society.

▦ 43 ▦

THE GREAT RAILROAD STRIKE,
PART II

O n July 20, 1877, B&O president John Work Garrett was
in a dour mood. A few days earlier, his beloved eighty-
five-year-old mother had passed away. Now, after he thought
he had put down a small labor disturbance in Martinsburg, his
trains had been stopped again at Cumberland. Garrett sum-
moned John Lee Carroll from his country estate and told the
governor he wanted federal troops. Carroll instead ordered
his national guard regiments to assemble and march to Camden Yards.

So it was that at 6:35 on that beautiful Friday evening,
bells all over the city, led by "Big Sam" at City Hall, sounded
the dreadful alarm—a riot was in progress. Curious working
people came out of homes and saloons to see what was afoot.
At 7:30, from far up Eutaw Street, came the unmistakable
thud and thunder of drums. The well-to-do crowd in front of
the Fifth Regiment Armory broke into polite applause as Baltimore's proud Fifth Regiment swung out onto Garden Street
behind its drum corps. They marched handsomely across
Madison to Eutaw, but there they confronted an awesome
sight. For Eutaw clear to the railroad yards was now packed
with thousands of angry working men. The workers went for
the guardsmen's rifles, and a riot started for real. Women hurled

rocks from upper-story windows and dropped a dozen militiamen in their tracks. As they came near the yards, the soldiers fixed bayonets and charged into the station.

Across town, the Sixth Regiment had an even worse time of it. Their armory was at Front and Fayette, in the heart of the factory district. A storm of rocks met them as they came out. Only after they had fired back, killing a few in the crowd, could they organize and begin their march.

On Baltimore Street though, another mob was waiting. Eyewitnesses said that as the troops came into view the crowd fell into a businesslike silence. Men and boys fingered the rocks in their pockets. The guardsmen reached them, and the crowd closed in. The fighting was hand-to-hand. By the time the Sixth finally made it to Camden Station, it had left behind ten dead rioters and scores of wounded—and half the regiment had deserted.

What was left of the national guard was now trapped inside Camden Station, along with Mayor Ferdinand C. Latrobe, Governor Carroll, the entire board of police commissioners, and a number of B&O officials, though not Garrett himself. Outside, fifteen thousand angry workers cheered and drank and threw stones through the windows.

"The working people everywhere are with us," one man told a Philadelphia reporter. "They know what it is to bring up a family on ninety cents a day, to live on beans and corn meal week in and week out, to run in debt at the stores until you cannot get trusted any longer, to see the wife breaking down under privation and distress, and the children growing sharp and fierce like wolves day after day because they don't get enough to eat."

Those children, the "wolves," had shown what they could do in Cumberland. Now they struck again. Three drunken boys jumped into the Chicago Express, got up steam, and drove it full speed into the yards, jumping off to watch as the locomotive rammed into some freights, tore up the platform on Lee Street, destroyed the dispatcher's office, and rolled upside down.

Rumor had it that the mob intended to burn all railroad property and then set fire to the city. Governor Carroll wired President Hayes for help, and Hayes sent what help he could. The crowd did burn some railroad stock, but at one o'clock, the riot died down as people went home to get some sleep. In subsequent days, as the strike moved on to Pittsburgh and still more bloodshed, police and federal troops restored order. On the surface, it appeared the anger in Baltimore had spent itself. Garrett declared victory. "We have the power," he said. "We have the public sentiment with us."

One Baltimore merchant disagreed. "The strike is not a revolution of fanatics willing to fight for an idea," he told another reporter. "It is a revolt of workingmen against low prices of labor which have not been accompanied with . . . low prices of food, clothing, and house rent."

He was close to the mark but not on it. "What in hell do I care if I do get killed!" a striker was heard to shout at the height of the rioting. "It might as well be so as to starve to death!"

Sources: Robert V. Bruce, *1877: Year of Violence* (Indianapolis: Bobbs-Merrill, 1959). For quotes, see letters to Jonathan King of the B&O Railroad, manuscript collection at the Maryland Historical Society.

⌘ 44 ⌘

GUS RICE

This is the story of a pirate. His name was Gus Rice, and he was born to poverty on the Eastern Shore. Rice learned to scrap and fight and somehow got by, working the water, doing odd jobs, picking peaches at thirty cents a day.

Then came the Oyster Boom of the 1860s and 1870s. Suddenly, Chesapeake oysters were on every table from New York to San Francisco. Sleepy little towns like Oxford and Crisfield began to look like Abilene and Dodge City. Rough, hard men from the oyster fleet staggered from saloon to saloon. Prostitutes beckoned in the streets. Murder was common. And Gus Rice got himself a dredge boat.

To keep order, Maryland established in 1870 an Oyster Police Force, led by a tall Kent Islander named Hunter Davidson. In January 1871, Rice sent two assassins aboard his police boat to kill him. Davidson barely escaped with his life, and Rice gained local notoriety.

In 1884, the oyster crop peaked at 15 million bushels, then dropped sharply. The dredgers had depleted the major oyster bars. Not to worry. "Thar's plenty arsters left up in the rivers," crowed a Crisfield packer, "and them drudgers'll git 'em."

The rivers, though, were by law restricted to men who tonged for oysters by hand. Gus Rice and his dredge boat *J. C. Mahoney* scoffed at it. In 1887 he led a squadron of pirate dredgers up the Chester River, running down tongers in their little canoes and dredging as they pleased. One group of tongers tried to protect themselves by building a fort with two small cannon. Rice and his men came ashore one night, drunk, and captured the lone sentinel asleep. They stripped him naked, sent him packing into the night, and shipped the guns aboard the *Mahoney*.

The next season, the pirates took on the Oyster Navy in open battle. In November 1888, fourteen pirate dredgers surrounded the police sloop *Eliza Hayward* in the Little Choptank and blasted it with two dozen shotguns. The *Hayward* fled to Oxford and wouldn't come out. A few nights later, Rice and his men were again busy in the Chester when they spotted a steamer in the fog. Taking it for a police gunboat, they opened fire. It turned out to be the passenger steamer *Corsica* of the Baltimore and Eastern Shore line. Accounts of bullets whizzing among terrified women and children were front-page news. Somebody had to do something about Gus Rice.

The job fell to Captain Thomas C. B. Howard, who just then was in Annapolis mounting a twelve-pound cannon on the Oyster Navy's strongest ship, the *Governor McLane*. On December 10, 1888, he steamed to the mouth of the Chester. Ahead he could see two pirate dredge boats acting as sentinels. Beyond them, Rice and the entire pirate fleet cruised back and forth across the oyster bars.

It was late afternoon. A dark gray sky hid his smoke as his boarding parties surprised the sentinel boats before they could sound an alarm. Howard loaded his cannon, got up full steam, and ploughed upriver in the fading daylight, straight toward the pirate fleet.

It was a trap. Before he could get off his first shot, the dredge boats parted and a voice cried out, "Join me, boys, in victory or in hell!" Barreling downriver came the *J. C. Mahoney* and eleven other dredge boats, lashed together to form a kind of raft, fortified with iron plate. Rice and thirty pirates opened fire. Howard got off four shots with his cannon, all into the rigging, before raft and steamer closed. At full speed he rammed the *Julia H. Jones,* then backed off and drove in again, this time hitting the *J. C. Mahoney.* The force of the blow carried the *McLane* into the center of the raft, where the Oyster Police began picking off pirates with their rifles. Frantically, the pirates unlashed themselves and sailed away, leaving the *Mahoney* and the *Jones* slowly sinking. The Oyster Navy had won a victory, but not the war. Gus Rice escaped.

A month later the pirate fleet mauled the police sloop *E. B. Groome* in a two-hour gunfight in the Choptank. The *Groome* fled to Cambridge, but the pirates pursued and boarded her there. They forced the captured policemen to work aboard the dredge boats for a time, then sent them off in a small rowboat.

And so it went to the end of the century. Oystermen complained that police were corrupt and drunk. Tongers worked at the risk of their lives. Bodies washed ashore at a rate of about one a week during oyster season. It was a world made for men like Gus Rice.

Source: John R. Wennersten, *The Oyster Wars of Chesapeake Bay* (Centreville, MD: Tidewater, 1981)

45

THE MAESTRO

Early in May 1891, Peter Ilyich Tchaikovsky, the great Russian composer, came to Baltimore in the company of the Boston Festival Orchestra to give a concert at the Lyceum on Charles Street. It was not love at first sight.

In the first place, he didn't want to be there at all. He was exhausted after four concerts in New York, including the opening of Carnegie Hall. And he loved New York, except on Sundays, when he couldn't get a drink. "This English Puritanism," he sighed, "irritates me very much." He got little sleep on the train, and when he arrived in Baltimore, nobody paid much attention.

"As usual, I was received at the hotel with cool contempt. Sitting alone in my room, I ... felt ... unhappy, chiefly because everyone around me speaks only English. I slept a little. Then I went into a restaurant for breakfast, and was quite annoyed because the waiter ... would not understand that I wished for tea and bread-and-butter only."

Rehearsal at the Lyceum didn't go well either. "The orchestra was small, only four first violins," he noted. Like the maestro himself, its members were tired of all the touring—and grumpy.

When Tchaikovsky substituted the Serenade for Strings for the scheduled Third Suite, the orchestra's young conductor made it clear he was not going to rehearse as much as the maestro thought necessary. That night, the Russian went onstage, expecting the worst, and managed to find it. "Everything went very well, but there was little enthusiasm in comparison with New York," he groused.

A post-concert dinner put on by Wilhelm Knabe, prominent and generous maker of pianos, was, Tchaikovsky said, "endlessly long," and he soon felt "quite worn out. A terrible hatred of everything seemed to come over me, especially of my two neighbors." By that he meant his dinner companions on either side, who happened to be instructors at the Peabody Conservatory.

But for all his griping, Tchaikovsky actually liked America. He loved American hospitality, which was given without the European expectation of something in return. "If only I were younger," he said, "I should very much enjoy my visit to this interesting and youthful country. I am convinced that I am ten times more famous in America than in Europe. . . . Several of my works, which are unknown even in Moscow, are frequently played here. I am a much more important person here than in Russia."

In New York, the exceedingly rich Andrew Carnegie had dazzled him. "He embraced me (without kissing me; men do not kiss over here)," he said, and "got on tiptoe and stretched his hand up to show my greatness, and finally made the whole company laugh by imitating my conducting. . . . I myself was quite delighted."

Even Baltimore had its good side. "It is a pretty, clean town," Tchaikovsky admitted. And the piano he'd played during the opening of Carnegie Hall had been made by his Baltimore dinner host, Wilhelm Knabe.

It goes without saying that musical geniuses can be hard to please. After all, here was a man who once described his own world-famous *1812 Overture* as "very loud and noisy." But what did Baltimore think of their temperamental Russian guest? Let's begin with that cranky conductor of the Boston Festival Orchestra, the fellow who frustrated Tchaikovsky and conducted most of the Lyceum concert that May afternoon. He was none other than Victor August Herbert, the Dublin-born rising star of the New York music scene. Herbert had played cello in the orchestra of Johann Strauss and would go on to create scores of operas, operettas, and compositions, including the "Baltimore Centennial March."

To the crowd at the Lyceum, though, Herbert was three-day-old fish, compared to Tchaikovsky. "It would have been far more satisfactory," the *Baltimore Sun* remarked, "if the afternoon had been devoted only to Tschaikowsky instead of introducing a bunch of scrappy selections." The small but appreciative audience gave the Russian maestro a rousing ovation and called him back onstage again and again. Tchaikovsky may have had mixed feelings about Baltimore, but Baltimore, then as now, knew what it liked.

Source: James Morfit Mullen, "Tchaikowsky's Visit to Baltimore," *Maryland Historical Magazine* 34 (1939): 41–45

▪ 46 ▪

THE HEIRESS AND
THE MEDICAL SCHOOL

In 1889, Daniel Coit Gilman, president of the new Johns Hopkins University, found himself with a serious problem. Sixteen years earlier, visionary Baltimore merchant Johns Hopkins had planned an institution in his city that would revolutionize American education and international medicine. He foresaw a university, a hospital, and a medical school that would combine research, clinical care, and medical training all in one place, and at his death in 1873 he left $7 million in B&O Railroad stock to make it possible. The university opened in 1876, but then the country entered a terrible depression. A few years later, John Work Garrett, who ran the B&O, died, and the railroad's stock plummeted, taking the endowment with it. The hospital finally opened to great fanfare in May of 1889, but there was no money for a medical school.

Gilman thought he would find the answer in a single rich man. Despite hard economic times, the country was full of them. Andrew Carnegie gave $100,000 to Bellevue Hospital Medical College in New York. A Vanderbilt donated half a million to New York's College of Physicians and Surgeons. Surely, Gilman thought, he could find another generous man among the titans of industry—some called them "robber barons"—to build his medical school, especially if he could name that school after himself. Gilman and his trustees scoured the country for such a man, but none came forward.

As it happened, Gilman was looking in the wrong place. The answer was right under his nose in Baltimore, and she wasn't a rich man but a very determined—and very wealthy—young woman. Mary Elizabeth Garrett, daughter of John Work Garrett, the B&O's iron-fisted "Railroad King" himself, had a better head for business than either of her brothers, who had been handed high places in Baltimore finance. She also had a personal axe to grind with Gilman. Her own education—the traditional course for wealthy young women—had been little more than fluff, and she had greatly wanted to study at the new Johns Hopkins University when it opened. But college wasn't for women—it would imperil their delicate natures—or so men thought at the time. Gilman flatly refused to admit her to the university.

He had picked the wrong woman to cross. When her father died and left Mary a third of an estate so vast its value defied calculation, she set about righting things. With the help of four young, wealthy friends—Julia Rogers, Mamie Gwinn, Bessie King, and M. Carey Thomas—she altered the future of education in Baltimore by building the Bryn Mawr School. Its purpose was to prepare young girls for the new women's college of the same name near Philadelphia, whose entrance requirements exceeded those of most men's colleges, and medical schools, too, for that matter.

When the question of the Hopkins medical school endowment came up, Mary and her friends saw their chance. If they could raise the money to endow it, they could demand that women be admitted on the same terms as men. While Gilman searched for his white knight, Mary and her friends organized a quiet, intense campaign to come up with the money first. After five years they had raised over $100,000 from women all across the country. Gilman reluctantly accepted their money and their condition of coeducation, but he then moved the finish line. Before it could open, the medical school now needed half a million dollars, he told them—five times what they had raised.

Initially crestfallen, Mary rebounded with the resilience and drive her father had so admired. A few days before Christmas 1892, with her own fortune rapidly disappearing in the economic swamp of the 1890s, Mary Garrett informed the hospital trustees that she would provide the rest of the money herself.

On October 3, 1893, three women stood beside fifteen men as Hopkins opened classes in the nation's first coeducational, graduate-level medical school. At Mary Garrett's insistence, the women in Baltimore and across the country, who had done more to improve medical education than their wealthy male counterparts, were honored with construction of the Women's Fund Memorial Building. In 1979 it was torn down to make way for the Preclinical Sciences Building. But the spirit of Mary Elizabeth Garrett remains, in the women who teach and study at a world-renowned institution.

Source: Kathleen Waters Sander, *Mary Elizabeth Garrett: Society and Philanthropy in the Gilded Age* (Baltimore: Johns Hopkins University Press, 2008)

▪ 47 ▪

THE PENNANT

In 1893 the nation fell into the worst depression it had ever seen. By the end of the year, a quarter of the railroads had collapsed, and a fifth of the country was out of work. In Baltimore, that winter was especially cold and cheerless. Not only were times hard, but the city's baseball team remained a doormat in the National League.

No one knew it, but, at least on the diamond, things were about to get better. Ned Hanlon had taken over the team and begun trading away the loafers and has-beens for promising players other teams had given up on. From Pittsburgh he got Joe Kelley, a handsome lady-killer with power but weak baseball skills. From the New York Giants came towering over-the-hill slugger Dan Brouthers, whose bat, they said, was the size of a wagon tongue. The Giants also tossed in a five-foot-four-inch infielder named Willie Keeler. Hanlon brought in Louisville's weak-hitting shortstop Hughey Jennings and St. Louis outfielder Walter Scott Brodie, the reckless son of a Confederate cavalry officer who practiced catching fly balls with his back to the plate. Since this was mobtown, the Orioles already had a formidable catcher in Wilbert Robinson, pitcher Sadie McMahon, and John McGraw. McMahon, an Irish roughneck with a wicked curve ball, had been acquitted of murder five years before. "Mugsy" McGraw was five feet seven inches of pure hostility and looked like he could commit murder any day.

In the spring of 1894, Hanlon took his team south to Macon, Georgia, for spring training. There he turned them into masters of speed and deception. By the time they left Macon, they could work the hit-and-run and double steal, bunt for hits, and were inventing the suicide squeeze. This was called "inside baseball," and nobody played it better.

Opening Day brought the New York Giants to town. Favored to win the pennant over the defending champions, the Boston Beaneaters, they were huge men with the league's best pitching. Hanlon had suggested that the city deck itself out in orange and black, the colors of the Baltimore oriole—and so it was, that glorious April day. As the sell-out crowd of more than fifteen thousand packed its way inside Union Park, an orchestra played "Be Kind, for They Are Orphans." Against the Giants' fireballing Amos Rusie, the Orioles in bright white uniforms, black stockings, and white caps unleashed their new game and won, eight to three. The economy was still terrible, but Baltimoreans could smile as their team took three straight.

That season was the finest Baltimore had ever seen. The Orioles won twenty-four of their last twenty-five and went into Cleveland needing only one more to win the pennant. After dropping the first game, they went up against an Ohio farm boy named Denton True Young, nicknamed "Cy" for "Cyclone." With the score tied five to five, Wee Willie Keeler smashed a hit deep to right center field and raced around the bases for an inside-the-park home run. The Orioles won fourteen to nine and clinched the first of three consecutive National League pennants.

The next few years saw the best baseball ever played anywhere. Joe Kelley broke hearts and hit for power. Hughey Jennings played shortstop the way no one has before or since.

"Mugsy" McGraw, sitting on the Oriole bench, hard by the third-base line, threw bats at the feet of opposing runners, and ostentatiously sharpened his spikes with a hand file.

Groundskeeper Thomas Murphy built up the baselines to help Oriole bunts stay fair, and let the weeds in right field grow high enough to hide a ball. That which Willie Keeler threw in to the cutoff man wasn't always the same ball the batter had hit.

Louisville rookie Honus Wagner got a single in his first time up against Baltimore, and his second time up connected again. "I might have had a triple," he said, "but Jack Doyle gave me the hip at first, Hughey Jennings chased me wide around second, and John McGraw blocked me off at third, then jammed the ball into my belly, knocking the wind out of me."

No one who ever played or watched the 1894 Orioles ever forgot them. And their glorious season clearly illustrates one of history's most important lessons: Hard times come and go, but in baseball, better times are only a year away.

Source: Burt Solomon, *Where They Ain't: The Fabled Life and Untimely Death of the Original Baltimore Orioles, the Team that Gave Birth to Modern Baseball* (New York: Free Press, 1999)

⬛ 48 ⬛

THE EVIL EMPIRE

Late in the summer of 1897, two teams vied for the National League pennant. Representing all that was good about the game of baseball, were the Boston Beaneaters, or as their very proper fans called them, the "Bostons." They stormed through August and into September, leaving other teams in the dust—all, that is, but one.

Down on the Chesapeake, in their hot, brawling, working-class city, the Baltimore Orioles had won three straight pennants, and a blistering record of their own kept them atop the standings looking for a fourth. Like their city, they played with no holds barred. Using what critics called "inside baseball," they bunted, singled, stole bases, mugged opposing runners, and abused opponents with language that horrified their northern rivals. One recent writer has gone so far as to call them the original "Evil Empire."

Ace pitcher Joe Corbett's brother was a prizefighter. Third baseman John McGraw—five feet seven inches of pure hostility—grabbed runners by the belt, hit them in the stomach, and sharpened his spikes with a gleam in his eye. Right fielder "Wee" Willie Keeler, who led the league with a stunning .430 batting average, hid spare balls in the tall outfield grass for those times when a hit got past him. Joe Kelley charmed the ladies with his devilish good looks and bedeviled pitchers with his bat. And Dirty Jack Doyle rattled pitchers and umpires alike with his knowledge of profanity.

To genteel Boston fans, the Orioles were corrupt and dirty shanty Irish, symbols of all that was wrong with the country. It was high time, they thought, to redeem the national game by taking down the Orioles. Across the nation, the sporting public agreed.

Late in September, Boston came to Baltimore for a three-game weekend series. A hundred and twenty of Boston's most dedicated fans, calling themselves the Royal Rooters, arrived on Friday by overnight train and checked into the Eutaw House. Then, carrying horns, kazoos, a bass drum, and a flag, they took their seats at Union Park. Surrounded by nearly fourteen thousand Orioles fans, they watched their beloved Bostons fall behind 2–0, then roar back to win. That night the aging wooden Eutaw House shook with their victory celebration, and the next morning they posed before the grand old hotel for a photograph with their team. That, said Boston center fielder Billy Hamilton, was tempting fate.

Sure enough, on Saturday the Orioles quickly took a 3–0 lead. Boston finally scored two in the seventh and, with two out and men on first and third, attempted a double steal. Oriole second baseman Heinie Reitz caught catcher Wilbert Robinson's high throw to second and threw to Doyle at first to get the retreating base runner. When the runner on third broke for home, Dirty Jack fired an off-target, one-hopper to the plate. The runner, who happened to be none other than the superstitious Billy Hamilton, did indeed meet fate in the person of the Orioles' mighty captain. With a spectacular play, Robinson corralled Doyle's throw and blocked the plate. Baltimore put the game out of reach and resumed its slim lead in the standings.

On Monday, an estimated thirty thousand fans, more than twice Union Park's previous record, jammed inside to see the series finale. Both teams played badly, but alas, this wasn't to be the Orioles' day. In a game that saw the lead change hands four times in four innings, and the two best-fielding teams in baseball combine for ten errors, Boston took an 8–5 lead into the seventh. Thirteen batters later, the rout was on. Final score: 19–10 Boston.

A Louisville newspaper cheered this "victory for clean, honest baseball. A throw-down to rowdyism." But those in Union Park witnessed something entirely different. Those "rowdy" Baltimore fans congratulated Boston players and serenaded the Royal Rooters by singing "Yankee Doodle," followed by "Dixie." Boston's band replied with "Maryland, My Maryland," and a period favorite, "The Blow that Nearly Killed Father." The largest crowd ever to see a baseball game, in a place once known as "Mobtown," presented the country with a lesson in, of all things, good sportsmanship.

Sources: Bill Felber, *A Game of Brawl: The Orioles, the Beaneaters and the Battle for the 1897 Pennant* (Lincoln: University of Nebraska Press, 2007); James H. Bready, *Baseball in Baltimore: The First 100 Years* (Baltimore: Johns Hopkins University Press, 1998)

49

MOUSE

By the segregated 1890s, American popular entertainment for white people hadn't grown much since the Civil War. Whites gathered for "medicine shows," sang "The Battle Hymn of the Republic" and "Swanee River," or read newspapers and the Bible. Mark Twain and the genteel William Dean Howells were the kings of literature. Men smiled wistfully on hearing "Casey at the Bat," audiences politely applauded Tchaikovsky, and theatergoers went to see Sherlock Holmes on stage. Couples danced to "The Beautiful Blue Danube" and swayed beneath paper lanterns to "After the Ball." But on the other side of the tracks, in the netherworld of American society, something new and powerful was brewing in the black parts of town.

On February 7, 1883, in a small house in a black neighborhood of segregated Baltimore, between the Belair Market and the Johns Hopkins Hospital, a little boy was born to a deeply devout woman and her hard-working husband, John Sumner Blake. The boy grew up small and frail, and his mother worried that he'd be taken by the evils of their working-class neighborhood—pool halls, saloons, and worst of all, brothels. She wanted him to be part of the church, and when he showed an interest in music, she bought him a pump organ.

The boy, though, had a mind of his own. Now and then he got into a little trouble. Once, when a pal threw a rope over a power line and brought it down in a shower of sparks, a woman pointed mistakenly and shouted, "That mouse-faced boy done it!" And so he gained a nickname: "Mouse."

"Mouse" did love music, but not his mother's kind. He liked what he heard at night, coming from the honky-tonks, and he loved the community's funerals. As a cortege marched to the cemetery, its band would play slowly and solemnly, but on the way back, it played those same pieces in a whole different way. The devil's music, his mother said, and forbade him to go. Mouse ran to the cemetery anyway just to hear the funeral band on the way back.

His mother was right. It was the devil's music. Its heart and soul lived in the city's brothels, where, since the Civil War, honky-tonk piano players like Jesse Pickett, Big Head Wilbur, Jack the Bear, and One Leg Willie Joseph were creating something called "ragtime." They composed their own tunes and competed to see who had the fastest hands. One night, Mouse stared through the window of a local brothel and watched the legendary Jesse Pickett's fingers dance across the keyboard. Pickett saw him watching and showed off a little. Mouse was hooked.

By the time he was fifteen and tired of school, he was good enough to get a job playing piano at Aggie Shelton's notorious "five dollar house." She guaranteed him an unheard-of three dollars a night if he didn't make that much in tips. To get there, he had to sneak out after his parents went to bed, pull on a rented pair of long pants at a nearby pool hall, and play until two or three in the morning. The girls and the customers loved him. Aggie Shelton never had to pay that guarantee.

But, of course, it couldn't last. One night, one of his neighbors passing by Aggie's heard the distinctive "wobble-wobble" he'd developed with his left hand and told his mother, who was waiting for him when he came home. His father would whip him, she promised, and all that day he waited. When John Sumner came in that night, he asked Mouse if it was true. The boy said, yes, it was. Father and son went upstairs.

In his son's room, before taking off his belt, his father asked, "What did you do with all the money?" The boy pulled back the oilskin covering the floor. Spread evenly so they wouldn't make any piles were fives, tens, and twenties, more cash than John Sumner had ever seen in his entire working life. "Mind if I take one of these?" he asked. They went downstairs, and John explained to his wife that their son was now embarked on a working life and should be allowed to continue.

And so he did, first at Aggie Shelton's, then at other brothels, then traveling shows, and finally New York, where he joined a growing group of musicians who were bringing the sound of the black underworld into the national lexicon. By then nobody called John Sumner Blake's son "Mouse" anymore. James Hubert Blake, the dapper young man who was about to change American music forever, would henceforth be known as "Eubie" Blake.

Source: Al Rose, *Eubie Blake* (New York: Schirmer, 1979)

▪ 50 ▪

GOLIATH

On the quiet Sunday morning of February 7, 1904, Art Summerfield, a wholesale clothing merchant from North Carolina who had stopped in Baltimore on his way to New York, was walking past the John E. Hurst & Co. building on German Street between Liberty and Hopkins Place when he spotted smoke coming from the fourth floor of the six-story building. About the same time, a private watchman and fire guard, Archibald McAllister, spotted smoke rising from the building's cellar grate and swirling upward in the steady southwest breeze.

Moments earlier, a heat-activated alarm in the Hurst building basement had gone off in the firehouse of Engine Company No. 15. Chains dropped in front of the horses' stalls, and with no one saying a word, the huge horses stepped quickly to their places at the wagons. Spiders, contraptions holding a full set of harness, dropped over each horse, and firemen quickly snapped their collars and buckled them into teams. A fireman stoked the firebox of No. 15's steam engine. Captain John Kahl gave the order to roll. The doors opened, and the huge teams thundered onto the cobblestones. All of twenty seconds had passed from the time the alarm sounded.

About a minute later, Kahl and Engine Company No. 15 were in front of the Hurst Building. The clocklike dial alarm on the outside wall told Kahl there was fire in the basement, and he thought to himself, this wasn't going to amount to much, probably just some smoldering rags. They'd all be back in the warmth of the firehouse in no time. But when his men—Harry Showacre, Guy Ellis, John Flynn and Jacob Kirkwood—broke in the door with a crowbar, the room was filled with smoke. "I knew we had a fire then," he said later.

Kahl sent one team of firemen to hose down the elevator shaft. He sent another with a chemical hose to the basement stairs. District engineer Lewin Burkhardt showed up, and Kahl told him to get help quickly. Just then, doors upstairs began banging shut. Kahl thought it was a watchman, until a low rumbling shook the building. Sensing real trouble, the firemen began to back out the door, but it was too late. "A sharp, splitting roar went up with reverberating thunder followed by a peculiar whistling noise like that made by a shrill wind," a newspaper reported the next day. This smoke explosion, or backdraft, blasted Kahl and his company right through the door and into the street. All except for Jacob Kirkwood, who slumped in a heap by the entrance. Kahl and a few men went back in and pulled him out—but not to safety. "I still don't know how we escaped being crushed to death," Kahl recalled later. "Brick and stone came thundering down, smashing No. 15-1 steam wagon. Flames shot all over the place, setting fire to other buildings, one sheet seared one of the horses pulling our water tower into position on Liberty Street."

The big white fire horse was named Goliath. As Engine Company No. 15's Hale Water Tower was moving up Liberty Street, part of a wall of the Hurst Company collapsed, and flame belched out onto the street, burning his right shoulder and flank. Goliath drove away from it, taking the water tower and its crew with him, out of reach of the falling stone, and saving their lives.

The fire that Captain Kahl thought was just a few smoldering rags spread quickly after the smoke explosion—and after misguided efforts to stop it by dynamiting buildings in its path worsened matters by carrying burning embers across the city. It burned for thirty hours and nearly destroyed all of Baltimore, giving rise to more than a few notable stories. One was that of Goliath. On September 13 he appeared at a parade to honor firefighters and celebrate the rebirth of the city. Fourteen hundred firefighters marched that day, from Baltimore and out-of-town companies that had come to the city's aid. Their engines shining with fresh paint and burnished brass, they made a dramatic spectacle. With them came Goliath, covered with garlands. As he passed the reviewing stand, observers noticed a wonderful thing—he appeared to understand and appreciate the crowd's wild ovation. It was understandable that they would think so. Goliath was now the most popular animal in Maryland.

Source: Peter B. Petersen, *The Great Baltimore Fire* (Baltimore: Maryland Historical Society, 2004)

51

THE JUNGLE

In 1906 a great earthquake rocked San Francisco. That same year, on the East Coast, a different sort of quake shook the world of books, and behind it was a determined young man from Baltimore.

Upton Sinclair was the son of a Virginia couple who had moved to the city after the Civil War. His mother had, or pretended to have, links to the Virginia aristocracy. His father drank too much. In 1888, ten years after Upton was born, the family moved to New York, where they lived in a succession of apartments and boarding houses, each less desirable than the last. Upton attended public schools, but though he was short, slightly built, and inclined to study, the tough Irish and Italian kids in his neighborhood never seemed to bother him. What affected him more were the times his family returned to Baltimore to visit his mother's sister, who had married John Randolph Bland, the richest man in the city. Their townhouse and country estate resembled something straight out of the Great Gatsby. The difference in circumstances was not lost on young Upton.

At fifteen, he became the youngest freshman at the City College of New York and at eighteen entered Columbia University, intent upon studying law. He soon gave that up to spend a summer in a cabin in the Canadian woods writing the great American novel. He met a girl instead, got married, and had a son. When his novel failed, he decided to write another, this one about the Civil War and the great theme of slavery.

To research it and save money, he built a cabin in the woods near Princeton University, so he could use the archives there. That winter was the coldest in years. His wife nearly committed suicide, and the finished novel didn't sell well. But that failure gave birth to an idea.

Looking around him, Sinclair saw that the old antebellum racial slavery had taken on a new form. Now it was economic. In the years since the war, the rich had gotten very rich indeed, while the poor worked, languished, and died in unrelieved misery. Social mobility had died, too. Class warfare was imminent.

Sinclair watched closely when, in 1904, workers in the Chicago stockyards struck against the so-called "beef trust," and were quickly crushed. He wrote a letter on their behalf and sent it to a Midwestern socialist newspaper, the *Appeal to Reason*, whose publisher then asked him if he'd like to write a book about American "wage slavery." That was it. In November 1904, Sinclair packed his bags and headed west, having read everything he could get his hands on about the meatpacking business. He spent the next six weeks walking through the plants themselves, disguised in workingman's clothes, carrying a lunch bucket, and seeing things no one except those condemned to work there were ever meant to see.

The result was a shocking book, entitled *The Jungle*. Sinclair described in sickening detail how diseased pigs and cattle made their way to the American table and how US soldiers in Cuba had died from eating beef treated with formaldehyde.

Readers gasped when he explained how packers used every part of the pig "except the squeal" in making sausage. He told how, occasionally, men blinded by steam fell into the rendering vats. "When they were fished out, there was never enough of them left to be worth exhibiting," he wrote. "Sometimes they would be overlooked for days, till all but the bones of them had gone out to the world as Durham's Pure Leaf Lard!"

Reaction was immediate. On reading the book, President Theodore Roosevelt launched an attack on the "beef trust." The Phillip D. Armour Company, Sinclair's thinly disguised target, tried to bribe Sinclair with a sum equal to about 6 million in today's dollars. Armour's lawyers tried to coopt his publisher, who angrily replied by giving the rights to European publishers. Soon, all the world was in an uproar. The slight, scholarly boy from Baltimore had written the book of his young life. Yet, once again, he had failed. Upton Sinclair had wanted people to see the plight of the American worker, but it soon became evident that what his readers cared about far more, was their food.

Sources: Anthony Arthur, *Radical Innocent: Upton Sinclair* (New York: Random House, 2006); Upton Sinclair, *The Jungle*

⊞ 52 ⊞

THE EXPLORER

A t 10:30 on the morning of April 7, 1909, Matthew Henson, a forty-two-year-old black man from Charles County, stood on the ice five hundred miles out in the Arctic Sea and watched the renowned explorer Robert E. Peary hobbling back to camp. The two men had worked together for twenty-two years, and this was their eighth attempt to discover the North Pole. Peary was determined to be the first to reach it. In 1892 he had broken his leg on an expedition but kept going until forced to turn back. In 1899 his feet froze in his boots, and nine toes had to be amputated. This time they were close, and they knew it. Peary had gone out a few miles to take the final readings, expecting to locate the exact spot himself. Yet, as he drew closer, Henson could see no sign of joy on the commander's face.

Five days before, they had set out to cover the last 132 miles. Each day a new sled and dog team had broken a trail over pressure ridges—some of them one hundred feet high. They had to watch for cracks in the ice that opened and closed with fatal unpredictability, into which dogs and men sometimes vanished. Each day the party grew smaller, as the previous day's lead sled peeled off and returned to the base camp. But they were moving fast. Henson had been making these marches for eighteen years and marked off the miles in his head and in his legs.

Peary's crippled feet forced him to ride the whole time in a dogsled, so he couldn't know what Henson now knew for certain—when they had stopped the previous night they had covered the entire 132 miles. Peary thought they had a little way still to go, but Henson reckoned they could stop looking for the Pole because they were standing on it.

Henson was probably the only American of his day to have made himself fluent in the "Eskimo" language, Inuit, and he knew something else, as well. He had overheard one of the Eskimos say how mean it was of Peary to take two Inuit and leave Henson behind as he went out to look for the Pole the next morning. In the racial calculus of the times, "Eskimos" counted for even less than black men, and Peary didn't want to share the glory with anyone.

Peary was fiercely competitive and a huge egotist, but in matters of science he was not a liar. As he and Henson approached one another, each dealt with the fact that they had reached the Pole the day before—together. Henson cheerfully held out his hand and said, "Well Mr. Peary, we are now at the Pole, are we not?"

Peary looked away. He covered his eyes with both hands as though they hurt and grumbled that he wasn't entirely certain they had reached the Pole. He hobbled off a short distance to take more measurements. Then, he ordered the American flag raised over the camp. Henson led the Eskimos in three cheers, and a few hours later they began the dangerous trek back to Greenland.

Along the way, Peary was cold as the ice itself. "From the time we knew we were at the Pole Commander Peary scarcely spoke to me," Henson wrote. "It grieved me very much."

As soon as the expedition made its triumphant return to New York, the arguments with doubters erupted. Peary defended his claim of having been the first man to reach the North Pole and gained wide fame. He was elected president of the all-white, all-male Explorers Club in New York. Henson, who had more than once saved Peary's life but who couldn't hope to join the Explorers Club, took odd jobs to support himself. Four years after he had stood on the top of the world, he was parking cars in a Brooklyn garage. When a black politician found him and expressed his outrage at this injustice, Henson just smiled and said there were no sled teams to drive in Brooklyn.

In 1920 a navy admiral, writing for the *National Geographic*, revisited the Peary expedition. "The Negro" he said of Henson, "was indispensable to Peary. . . . With years of experience equal to that of Peary himself, an expert dog driver, a master mechanic, physically strong and most popular with the Eskimos, talking the language like a native, clean, full of grit, he went to the Pole with Peary because he was easily the most efficient of all Peary's assistants." But this was the United States at the beginning of the twentieth century, and Matthew Henson wasn't permitted to join the National Geographic Society either.

Source: Floyd Miller, *Ahdoolo: The Biography of Matthew A. Henson* (New York: Dutton, 1963)

▪ 53 ▪

THE AVIATOR

As the twentieth century dawned, nothing so captured the human imagination as the idea of conquering the mysteries of flight. In the United States and Europe, daring young men launched themselves skyward in flimsy machines of wood and cloth that were held together with nothing more than a little wire—and faith. Among the first was Hubert Latham, a young Frenchman who was equal parts Indiana Jones and Inspector Clousseau and who, for a few glorious years, held the world spellbound.

Born in 1883 to wealthy parents, Latham grew up in a chateau outside Paris. As a young man, he was tall and slender and spoke perfect English. After briefly attending Oxford he fulfilled his military service in Paris, then set out to satisfy his need for adrenalin. With a cousin, he crossed the English Channel—in a balloon, at night. In 1905 he raced a motor yacht in the Monaco Regatta, led an expedition to explore what is now Ethiopia the following year, and in 1908 departed for the Far East.

On his return, he went to Le Mans to watch Wilbur Wright demonstrate his aeroplane for the French military and immediately began looking around for someone who would teach him to fly. As it happened, a distant cousin owned the Antoinette Company, which had made the engines for the motor yachts Latham raced, and now the company was getting into the aircraft business. In no time he became Antoinette's best pilot.

What to do next? Well, the *London Daily Mail* had offered a thousand pounds to the first pilot to fly across the English Channel, but crossing the channel was no easy thing to do. Aircraft engines had to be light and often lost power after half an hour or so. Still, how could a man like Latham refuse?

On July 19, 1909, he took off from Cap Blanc-Nez and thereby became the first man to *attempt* to cross the channel. Eight miles later, when his engine failed, he became the first man to land on water. As his Antoinette bobbed in the waves, he sat in the cockpit, calmly lit a cigarette, and waited to be rescued.

Before he could procure a new plane and attempt a second flight, rival Louis Blériot beat him to Dover and the thousand pounds. But Latham wasn't finished. In succeeding months he flew demonstrations across Europe, crashed repeatedly, and at Blackpool in Britain became the first man to fly backward when he foolishly took off into a forty-mile-an-hour gale. By 1910 he was world famous, which brings us to Maryland.

To coincide with an air show at Halethorpe, the *Baltimore Sun* offered Latham $5,000 if he would fly over the city so that Baltimoreans could "witness the most remarkable scientific triumph of the present age." A bedridden Ross Winans, grandson of the Baltimore railroad tycoon, offered Latham an additional $500 to fly over his house at 1215 St. Paul Street.

So it was that shortly after noon on November 7, 1910, Latham took off from Halethorpe and headed east toward Fort McHenry, then weaved back and forth across the city. Beneath him church bells pealed, workers looked up in awe, and patients at Johns Hopkins Hospital struggled to their windows. On St. Paul Street, a delighted Ross Winans watched from his bedroom as the single-wing Antoinette slowly circled his house.

Twenty-five miles and forty-two minutes later, having pushed his engine to the limit, Latham landed at Halethorpe. But of course this was nothing for a man who had landed in the Channel, flown backwards, and become the first to shoot a duck from an airplane. Latham sat in his cockpit with the engine running and lit another cigarette while mechanics pulled him into the hangar. Then, with admirable Gallic insouciance, he turned to a waiting crowd of eager reporters and said, "Not a word until I have eaten lunch."

A year later Latham undertook another expedition on behalf of the French government, this one to the Congo, but this time he didn't return. The official report was that he had been gored by a rampaging buffalo, but there were others who said he died at the hands of his own porters. We'll never know. We know only that Baltimoreans remembered his flight as they remembered the Great Fire of 1904, and the lucky few to whom he had given autographed one-dollar bills never entertained a thought of spending them.

Sources: Maryland Historical Society's library blog, http://mdhslibrary .wordpress.com/2013/03/; BBC, http://news.bbc.co.uk/2/hi/uk_news /magazine/8080077.htm

▦ 54 ▦

DIAMOND JIM

In 1856 an Irish saloonkeeper on the New York waterfront named his newborn son for the Democratic presidential candidate that year, James Buchanan. The boy dropped out of school early to work as a hotel bellhop, took another job with the New York Central Railroad, and then went to work selling railroad equipment during the boom years of America's Gilded Age. When he started out, an older salesman advised him, "Make people like you." A large diamond glittered on the man's lapel. "And always look like you've got lots of money." Jim Brady took the advice to heart. When fat commissions started rolling his way, he bought diamonds by the pocketful and wore them on his lapels, vest buttons, cufflinks, rings, and pocket watch. He even put a three-carat gem in the handle of his walking stick. Soon everyone was calling him "Diamond Jim."

Besides money, he had two passions. One was Broadway. He became a "first nighter," showing up down front on opening night and later backstage with flowers and candy for the actresses. His other passion was food. Jim Brady had possibly the largest appetite of anyone in an age of enormous eaters. Breakfast might consist of a beefsteak, chops, eggs, flapjacks, fried potatoes, hominy, corn bread, and a pitcher of milk. Lunch began with a couple of dozen oysters, clams, deviled crabs, a broiled lobster or two, another steak, salad, two kinds of pie, and finally ended with a box of chocolates. Hard as it is to be-lieve, dinner with clients or an actress was often lobsters, turtle soup, broiled fish, canvasback duck, terrapin, fresh vegetables, pies, fruits, nuts, bonbons, and chocolate mints. One restau-rant owner called Diamond Jim Brady the best twenty-five customers he ever had.

But one night in April 1912, Jim got into bed with severe stomach pains and difficulty urinating. The next morning, his doctor rushed him by special train to Johns Hopkins, where the first doctors to examine him found a large kidney stone and a stomach that was an astonishing six times the normal size. While staff reinforced a bed and an operating table to hold a man who weighed well over three hundred pounds, they called in Dr. Hugh H. Young, a rising star in urology. Young's examination revealed diabetes, Bright's Disease, high blood pressure, inflammation and obstruction of the prostate, and coronary artery disease. Young said he could remove the kid-ney stone with a new procedure, but he didn't want to do it because the risk of postoperative infection was high, and he was about to leave for a conference in Europe. Brady insisted he operate right away. Four days later, with Brady's tempera-ture rising at an alarming rate, Young left for New York.

Representatives of the city's finest hotel met his train and escorted Young and his family and servants to its best suite of rooms, all "compliments of Mr. Brady." That night a private car drove them down Broadway so Young's children could see the lights of the Great White Way. The next day it took them to the docks.

Their staterooms, stocked with flowers, chocolates, wines, and liqueurs, were far better than what Young had booked and again, "compliments of Mr. Brady." "All this from a man I had known for only a few days," Young wrote, "and who . . . was so sick . . . I was not sure he would recover."

But Brady did recover, in his own way. Disliking hospital food, he had his meals brought in from the Belvedere Hotel, and before he left, he gave each nurse at Hopkins—fifty in all—a two-carat diamond ring.

"They . . . handed me back a newly lined, high-powered, . . . stomach," he told an adoring New York press, adding that he could eat a whole bull moose if someone cooked it for him. When Brady returned to Baltimore for a checkup, Young just happened to mention that he needed funding to start a urological institute. Brady pledged $200,000 for the project.

Five years later, Diamond Jim Brady died peacefully in his sleep. With no wife or children, much of his fabulous wealth went to charitable causes, including $300,000 to Hugh Young at Johns Hopkins, who built the James Buchanan Brady Urological Institute. To this day the legacy of "Diamond Jim" still sparkles in that world-renowned medical constellation.

Source: H. Paul Jeffers, *Diamond Jim Brady: Prince of the Gilded Age* (New York: John Wiley and Sons, 2001)

▣ 55 ▣

THE BABE

Early in the spring of 1914, the manager of the Terrapins, the Federal League team in baseball-crazy Baltimore, got a call from a bartender insisting his kid be given a tryout. The manager reminded the bartender that the Terrapins were in first place, and told him he already had enough talent and didn't want a rookie.

As it happened, though, Jack Dunn, who managed the team that played across Twenty-Ninth Street from the Terrapins—the scrappy, ne'er-doing-very-well minor-league Orioles—had heard about the kid and had gone out to St. Mary's Industrial School to see him play. The boy was huge—over six feet and growing—and a discipline problem. But he sure could play baseball. He pitched left handed, played outfield, and even played catcher with the only thing available, a right-hander's mitt. Dunn signed him.

The Orioles were headed south to Fayetteville, North Carolina, for what passed as spring training in those days. Carolina weather was a bit warmer than Baltimore's, though just as unpredictable, but teams found enough time and opponents to more or less get ready for the season in April. Dunn arranged to play some local teams and staged intrasquad games for revenue, but he also knew that the world-champion Philadelphia Athletics would soon be passing through nearby Wilmington on their way up from Florida.

The new kid, named Ruth and called "Little George" by his family and the disciplinarians at St. Mary's, was enchanted by Fayetteville. It was his first trip away from home, his first train ride, his first hotel, and, at the hotel, his first time in an elevator. "I got to some bigger places than Fayetteville after that," he would say later, "but darn few as exciting." He loved the players' practical jokes and doubtless howled when somebody tethered a horse overnight in the hotel lobby. Worldly teammates figured him for a rube and good-naturedly began calling him "Babe."

On March 7, George Ruth was playing shortstop in an intrasquad game when he unleashed a towering home run over the right fielder's head. "I hit it as I hit all the others," he told local reporters, "by taking a good gander at the pitch as it came up to the plate, twisting my body into a backswing and then hitting it as hard as I could swing." "The ball just disappeared," gushed the batboy's brother. "I haven't seen that ball yet." Back in Baltimore, newspapers ran headlines on the order of "Homer by Ruth Feature of Game," and "Ruth Makes Mighty Clout."

Between bouts of bad weather, Ruth played and pitched well for the Orioles in three wins over the lowly Philadelphia Phillies of the National League, and late in March the team left Fayetteville to play their way north. They arrived in Wilmington just as Connie Mack, Frank "Home Run" Baker, Eddie Collins, "Chief" Bender, and the rest of the champion Athletics sauntered into town. Everyone wanted to see the two teams play. Oriole pregame publicity ignored George Ruth, concentrating instead on hot new rookie phenom, "Cousin George" Twombly.

As thousands of fans paid fifty cents each to crowd into Sunset Park in Wilmington, Jack Dunn named Ruth his starting pitcher. The rookie might have been nervous had he any idea what he was going up against. The Athletics hammered him for thirteen hits, four by "Home Run" Baker. At one point an exasperated Ruth looked over at his manager and shouted, "Dunnie, who's that big stiff on third base? I can't seem to get him out." At the plate, Ruth went 0 for 4.

But a curious thing happened. Although the superbly talented Athletics hit Ruth hard and often, they couldn't score. The hits were wasted, said a Wilmington paper, because in the clutch "the batters could not connect with Ruth's well regulated supply of benders." The final score surprised everyone: Orioles 6, Athletics 2.

The Orioles left Carolina for Baltimore, and a few months later, in need of money, sold pitcher George Herman Ruth and two other players to Boston for $20,000. One afternoon before he left, Ruth lashed a dead leather ball into the centerfield fence so hard the rebound rocketed all the way back to the second baseman. A force of nature was about to hit major league baseball, in the form of a big, fearless kid from Baltimore's St. Mary's Industrial School, a kid called "Babe."

Sources: Jim L. Sumner, "Babe Ruth's North Carolina Spring: The Tarheel Perspective," *Maryland Historical Magazine* 86 (1991): 80–89; James H. Bready, *Baseball in Baltimore: The First 100 Years* (Baltimore: Johns Hopkins University Press, 1998)

⊞ 56 ⊞

TITANIC

On April 10, 1912, shortly after noon, RMS *Titanic* of the White Star Line, representing the height of Edwardian engineering and luxury, left Southampton on her maiden voyage to New York. Since how one traveled was every bit as important as where one went, the men and women in her first-class cabins were the cream of American and British society. Among them were Philadelphia banker William E. Carter; his wife, the former Baltimore debutante Lucille Polk; their two children; and two servants. A year earlier they had gone to Europe with their polo ponies, and now they were coming home in style. When not taking in the view from the upper decks, Mr. Carter and his popular wife, who some said looked like a perfect Gibson girl, could be found chatting with John Jacob Astor over coffee, mingling with prominent members of Philadelphia society, or passing the time with J. Bruce Ismay, the chairman of the White Star Line.

All went splendidly until 11:40 on their fifth night out, when the *Titanic*, cruising through a calm sea at just over 22 knots, passed too close to an iceberg and suffered a gash down a quarter of her starboard side below the waterline. Most passengers felt only a slight change in the ship's vibrations, until the captain stopped the engines. Most of those in first class felt nothing at all. Some caroused in the ice that had fallen onto the deck or playfully put pieces of it into their drinks.

They didn't know the wireless operator was sending a distress signal, but if they had, they wouldn't have worried. *Titanic*'s new watertight doors and superior construction would keep her afloat even though damaged. As one crewman told a woman when the decks began to slant ever so slightly forward, "God himself couldn't sink this ship."

Soon thereafter, though, the crew called everyone on deck with their lifebelts and began to lower the boats. William Carter told Lucy to "Get up and dress yourself and the children," then went looking for other Philadelphians. The unwritten Edwardian code for gentlemen held that women and children went into the boats first. Wearing a diamond horseshoe stickpin on her blouse but leaving the rest of her jewelry behind where it would be safer, Lucy Carter steered her children into Boat Number 4 on the port side and took up an oar. Meanwhile, William Carter had gone to the starboard side and joined company chairman Ismay. There were fewer people there, and when no more women or children came forward, they climbed into a partially filled boat themselves. Despite the fact that there were still scores of women and children in second and third class aboard, the boat was lowered to the water. Apparently, they were not a gentleman's concern.

At 2:20, with the band still playing, *Titanic*'s bow plunged, and her stern rose high in the air. Those still aboard reached for something to hold onto or jumped into the sea as she slowly sank by the bow. The temperature of the water was thirty-one degrees.

It was nearly morning before rescue ships arrived to pick up the lifeboats. The screams and cries for help from those left behind had long since fallen silent. At 2902 St. Paul Street in Baltimore, Lucy's father was assuring reporters, "It is usual in such cases that the first-class passengers are given the preference. . . . Mrs. Carter must be among that number." He was right. At eight o'clock, Boat Number 4 came alongside the Cunard steamer *Carpathia*, and a shivering and exhausted Lucy Carter struggled aboard. Leaning on the rail, nonchalantly watching the rescue was her husband. He'd just had a jolly good breakfast, he told her. Then he added that he hadn't thought she would make it.

A British court of inquiry later determined that the boat carrying J. Bruce Ismay and William E. Carter had left a full fifteen minutes before Lucille's. A humiliated Ismay left the company and died in self-imposed exile in 1937. Suspicion that he had behaved most disgracefully also cast a shadow upon one William Carter. In 1914, Lucy sued for divorce, charging "cruel and barbarous treatment and indignities to the person." Not surprisingly, she won.

Sources: Walter Lord, *A Night to Remember* (New York: Holt, Rinehart and Winston, 1955), and Lord, *The Night Lives On* (New York: William Morrow, 1986). Initial inaccurate reports of Carter and the sinking of the *Titanic* are online at www.encyclopedia-titanica.org/titanic-survivor /lucile-carter.html.

57

THE GREAT BATHTUB HOAX

D ecember 20 marks an important anniversary in American history, one that we appreciate year-round and one with a prominent Baltimore connection. The story begins sometime in the 1830s, when a Cincinnati grain and cotton merchant named Adam Thompson found himself in England on business. A few years earlier, in 1828, Lord John Russell and a small group of British enthusiasts had begun using an undersized contrivance called a "bath tub." Somehow, Thompson learned of it and acquired the strange new habit of taking a daily bath. He then brought this preposterous idea home with him to Cincinnati.

Thompson was a successful man, and he lived in a large, well-made house. That was fortunate, because the bathtub he designed was much bigger than Lord Russell's puny tin basin. For one thing, Thompson thought a man should be able to sit in it. For another, he figured bathing would be much simpler if a maid didn't have to lug water into the house. Thompson attached a large six-man hand pump to his well and pumped water up to a tank in his attic. From there, two pipes ran down to what came to be called the "bath room."

The first was a direct line and provided cold water. The second detoured into the chimney, where it coiled around the flue, and provided water heated by the cooking fire in the kitchen.

The pipes emptied into a splendid new device put together by one James Cullness, the best cabinetmaker in Cincinnati. Constructed of elaborately polished Nicaraguan mahogany, "it was nearly seven feet long and fully four feet wide. To make it watertight, the interior was lined with sheet lead, carefully soldered at the joints. The whole contraption weighed about 1,750 pounds, and the floor of the room in which it was placed had to be reinforced to support it."

At eight o'clock on the morning of December 20, 1842, Adam Thompson climbed into his marvelous new tub and took a cold bath. Later that afternoon he took another, this one with water heated to a comfortable 105 degrees. Delighted with the results, on Christmas Day he invited a number of gentlemen to dinner and showed off his new invention. Four of them risked life and health and tried it, one after another. The next day, word of what had come to Cincinnati hit the newspapers, and soon a violent dispute was underway.

Everyone knew that bathing was dangerous. Philadelphia immediately considered an ordinance prohibiting bathing between November 1 and March 15—it failed by only two votes.

Virginia laid a thirty-dollar tax on bathtubs, and Hartford, Providence, Charleston, and Wilmington, Delaware, raised the water rates for those using them. Boston made bathing illegal except on medical advice.

Bathtubs were the province of the rich for a few years until a Brooklyn plumber named John F. Simpson designed one, made of zinc, that was far more affordable. Bathing quickly began to catch on. By 1850 there were a thousand bathtubs in New York City, and one or two in every hotel. Then, Dr. Oliver Wendell Holmes himself came out in favor of bathing, and the American Medical Association declared it a harmless practice. The final push came from none other than Millard Fillmore. In March 1850, while still vice president and stumping in Cincinnati, he visited the original Thompson bathtub. That July, when President Zachary Taylor died after eating too many cherries, Fillmore became president and shortly thereafter ordered a bathtub constructed in the White House. Bathing had come to the United States.

By now you must wonder what this has to do with Baltimore. It is simply this: The history of the American bathtub and all its wonderful detail comes to us courtesy of one Henry Louis Mencken. The story first appeared in the *New York Evening Mail* on December 28, 1917, and for years afterward it was cited by academic and medical authorities, all of whom were completely unaware that they had been hoodwinked. You see, Henry Louis Mencken, merry prankster that he was, had made the whole thing up.

Source: H. L. Mencken, *A Mencken Chrestomathy: His Own Selection of his Choicest Writings* (New York: Vintage, 1982)

☒ 58 ☒

THE LAST MAN

Late in the morning of November 11, 1918, wild rumors began to surge through the trenches stretching across France and Belgium from the English Channel to the Swiss border. Couriers rushed forward with the news—a general ceasefire would begin at 11 a.m. The Great War was going to end.

German, French, and British soldiers were elated. Exhausted after four long years of bloody, pointless fighting, they were now falling victim to a new enemy, a strange and deadly influenza. The news of the ceasefire brought immense joy and relief. German soldiers rose above their parapets, clowning, dancing, and shouting, "Der Krieg ist über!"—the war is over.

Not so the Americans. General John J. Pershing, commander of the American Expeditionary Force, didn't care for the idea of a ceasefire. That morning his division commanders relayed orders that until eleven o'clock, operations would be "pressed with vigor." At eleven, "our line will halt in place, and no man will move one step backward or forward." Until then, the attacks would go on.

One of the units pressing on with vigor that morning was the 313th Regiment, known as "Baltimore's Own," since that was home for most of its men. Among them was a handsome young man in his early twenties with a clipped mustache that made him look more like a British officer than an American doughboy. His name was Henry Gunther, and he lived in East

Baltimore, where many families, including his own, had relatives in Germany. Before the war he had worked as a bank clerk and become engaged to a young German-American woman. He had also felt the sting of anti-German sentiment in the city and hated to leave his neighbors and his fiancée to face it without him.

In France he was promoted to sergeant, until the censors intercepted his letter advising a friend that conditions were so bad he should stay out of the army. The army quickly demoted him to private. To remove this humiliating stain on his record, he volunteered for the dangerous job of runner, carrying messages from headquarters to the front, and was soon wounded so severely that he could have come home had he wanted to. He chose to stay.

By November 11, the regiment had been engaged in heavy fighting for two straight months, but at 9:30 that morning they fixed bayonets and went over the top one last time, into a marsh and toward a tiny spot on the map, Ville-devant-Chaumont.

Fog engulfed them, so heavy that their supporting machine-gun company soon had no idea where they were. Then, the German artillery opened up. Most of the shells sank harmlessly in the mud, but here and there one exploded and killed someone. The regiment kept on.

Just before eleven, German machine gunners defending Ville-devant-Chaumont were about to celebrate the war's end when shadowy figures suddenly appeared in the mist. The Germans watched in amazement. An attack made no sense. When the Americans kept coming they fired a warning. The doughboys fell to the ground as the bullets whizzed over their heads, and both sides thought that was the end of it. The time was 10:58.

Then one lone American stood up. Henry Gunther thrust his bayonet forward and ran toward the German lines. His friends called for him to stop. So did the Germans, but Henry kept going. No one knew why. Perhaps he wanted one last chance to prove himself to his family and neighbors, or to those who harassed them. The Germans shrugged and reluctantly fired another short burst—lower this time. Henry staggered and collapsed into the mud. It was 10:59. One minute later, the trenches erupted in laughter and song and tears of disbelief. The war was over.

Henry's final act of bravery, or desperation, regained him his lost honor. He was awarded the Distinguished Service Cross and restored to the rank of sergeant, posthumously. Henry also unknowingly claimed another distinction. In the six hours between the *time* the armistice had been signed at five o'clock that morning and the ceasefire at eleven, 2,738 men had died. Henry Gunther of East Baltimore was the last of them, the last man to die in the War to End All Wars.

Source: Joseph E. Persico, *Eleventh Month, Eleventh Day, Eleventh Hour: Armistice Day, 1918, World War I and Its Violent Climax* (New York: Random House, 2004)

▦ 59 ▦

MARYLAND, THE FREE STATE

At midnight, on January 16, 1920, the Volstead Act, the Eighteenth Amendment to the Constitution, banning the sale or consumption of alcohol, went into effect. In hotel bars, waterfront saloons, and roadside taverns all across the state, bartenders gave away half-empty bottles and glumly closed their doors. Working people, travelers, veterans returning from France, and society bigwigs alike all faced the sad truth. After decades of crusading, the temperance movement had won the day. The hopeful looked ahead and wondered what the great experiment would bring. Those who saw the glass half full waited for the heavy hand of "dry tyranny" to enter their lives.

They didn't wait long. H. L. Mencken, who had warned that Prohibitionists were "trying to ram their peruna down the national gullet," got an early taste of it on the way to the New York office of the *Smart Set* magazine. The red cap who picked up his bag at Pennsylvania Station told him it felt a little heavy and nodded toward a couple of men standing in the shadows. Detectives, he said, looking for gentlemen carrying a secret bottle or two. Anyone suspicious they took downstairs and searched. The guilty went to jail.

Mencken had heard of federal agents waking people on sleeping cars and rifling their possessions in search of contraband booze. Even ladies' luggage wasn't safe. "This week I seen them nail about thirty gentlemen," the red cap said, but added, "don't worry, I know how to carry it . . . so's it looks light."

Marylanders shared Mencken's outrage. The state attorney general absolved the state police of any responsibility to enforce the law, and most Maryland jurisdictions followed suit. When President Warren G. Harding, over lunch at a national governors' conference, lectured the governors on their duty to strictly enforce the law, Governor Albert C. Ritchie himself stood up and fired back that Marylanders had handled the temperance issue quite well for several centuries, thank you, and didn't need this "unnecessary and drastic federal infringement on their State and personal rights." Ritchie and his state became a national rallying point against dry tyranny. In 1923, Ritchie won reelection in a landslide, and the phrase "Maryland, the Free State," became a local battle cry.

On the lighter side was John Philip Hill, a young Baltimore lawyer, war veteran, and Republican congressman from a Democratic, working-class district. When the *Evening Sun* asked all politicians where they stood on Prohibition, Hill went the paper one better. Noting that farmers, but not city people, were allowed to make wine and cider from their fruit, he renamed his Franklin Street house "Franklin Farms," planted a few grape vines and apple trees in his back yard, and let nature take its course.

As the yield in his cider rose, he complained to the paper that his fruit—not he—was breaking the law and asked federal agents for advice. They arrested him. In US District Court, a jury—doubtless knowledgeable—tasted his wine, which was now above 12 percent alcohol, and with a wink pronounced it "not intoxicating in fact." Then Hill's district reelected him in yet another landslide.

Maryland had its share of smugglers and rumrunners, but Baltimore never became another Chicago. Instead of barricaded speakeasies, Baltimore had restaurants that not so secretly announced that they offered illegal drinks by displaying the lighted sign of a red crab in the window. Here and there a basement explosion marked where some home brewer had miscalculated, but alcohol was freely available. After all, the US Industrial Alcohol Corporation at Curtis Bay produced millions of gallons annually, and much of it found eager buyers at three dollars a jug.

And so the Jazz Age danced on in Maryland, understated, civilized, and fiercely defiant, as befitted the Free State. The dry crusade seethed as young men bought fast cars and raccoon coats, young women bobbed their hair and smoked in public, and Marylanders everywhere raised a glass against tyranny, beneath the sign of the "red crab."

Source: Various, including Robert J. Brugger, *Maryland, A Middle Temperament* (Baltimore: Johns Hopkins University Press, 1988), 470–71 (John Philip Hill), and Marion Elizabeth Rodgers, *Mencken: The American Iconoclast: The Life and Times of the Bad Boy of Baltimore* (New York: Oxford University Press, 2005)

⸙ 60 ⸙

LEANDER

In 1920 the premier Olympic sport was not swimming or track and field but crew, eight men rowing a slender shell down a river course of two thousand meters at a speed of eighteen knots. And nobody owned crew like Great Britain. English teams had not lost a single boat race they'd entered since the Olympics began again in 1892. As the world's athletes convened in Antwerp to meet for the first time since the Great War, England called upon its Leander Boat Club, whose emblem, a pink hippopotamus, indicated that they were indeed kings of the river. The pink stood for their original colors of red and white, run together some time in the century since their founding. With Leander going, English rowing families expected a short, one-word cablegram from Belgium: "Gold."

But on the Chesapeake, there were those with other ideas. A few years earlier a crusty Cape Codder had come to Annapolis to coach the Navy crews. Richard Glendon did not have the flower of English manhood to work with but rather farmboys and grocers' sons from all across the United States. Glendon noticed immediately that his men were bigger and stronger than the average oarsman and required a different kind of boat than the slender shells used in England and imported to American rowing clubs, so he designed one that was broader and heavier. To take advantage of their strength, he widened the oar's blade, shortened the stroke, and called the whole thing his "American System." During the winter, his middies trained inside. In the frigid winds of March, they moved outdoors to begin their grueling training on the Severn.

They looked nothing like the English, who pulled together in a symphony of long, graceful strokes. The press described Glendon's crew as motley, homely, and awkward. But after a narrow loss to mighty Syracuse, the Navy crew out-rowed Penn, Harvard, Yale, Princeton, Columbia, and the Union Boat Club, then went on to win the American Henley Regatta in Philadelphia. So great was national delight in their progress that they were given permission to compete in the Olympic trials in July. Under a bright New England sun in Worcester, Massachusetts, Navy set a course record, avenged the earlier loss to Syracuse, and set their sights on Belgium.

Across the Atlantic, the best of the great rowing families from Oxford and Cambridge awaited them with the confidence of proven champions. While the Americans worked out the kinks after several weeks at sea, Leander trained at home and gave themselves a formal send-off dinner in their clubhouse at Henley on the Thames. They arrived in Antwerp only to find poor accommodations and, worse, that the race had been moved to Vilvoorde, eight miles away. Still, while the runners and swimmers competed, Leander went about their preparations unfazed, and when the rowing finally began, they swept easily through their bracket.

So did Navy.

The two teams met on the last day of the games, before the largest crowd yet to see an Olympic event. Cyg Swann, one of the greatest rowers ever to come out of Cambridge, warned his mates not to take the Americans lightly, but they assured themselves that, with their style, strength, and superior oarsmanship, they would beat these big, awkward men.

At 5 p.m. on Sunday, August 29, the shells glided to the starting line. A cannon boomed, the starting flag dropped, and the crowd roared as the boats jumped forward. Leander set a blistering early pace of forty-one strokes per minute and at one thousand meters led by two-thirds of a length. They increased to forty-two, but to their shock and amazement, Navy didn't fade as expected. The Americans began to close. Oxford, Cambridge, and a century of English tradition dug in for the finish, but at seventeen hundred meters, Navy had drawn even. With thirty meters to go, the Navy coxswain called for ten strokes full out. His shell surged forward and sped across the line half a length ahead.

That evening, the young English gentlemen visited the American tents to congratulate the victors and talk about the race. There would be no one-word cablegrams, and they would face a critical press at home, but, having just smashed the Olympic record by more than seven full seconds, they were still the best Britain had ever sent onto the water. Unfortunately, thanks to a determined, unorthodox crew from Annapolis, they were no longer the best in the world.

Source: Susan Saint Sing, *The Wonder Crew: The Untold Story of a Coach, Navy Rowing, and Olympic Immortality* (New York: St. Martin's, 2008)

▦ 61 ▦

THE SCHNEIDER CUP RACE

OF 1925

In 1913, Jacques Schneider, a French aeronautical pioneer, organized an annual race to spur the development of seaplanes. A Frenchman won that first prize of 90,000 francs at Monaco by flying at the breakneck speed of sixty-one miles per hour. World War I suspended the competition, but with the 1920s came the golden age of airplane racing. The Americans, whose government had funded the Curtiss Airplane Company, offered to host the 1925 Schneider Cup race near Baltimore. Britain and Italy began work on new planes, while the Americans pursued speed records with their Curtiss Racers.

Early in October, a group of daring pilots and odd-looking planes converged on Bay Shore Park to race for the Schneider Cup. At the end of a trolley line fourteen miles southeast of Baltimore, Bay Shore had a beach and a boardwalk, but no one had thought to put up hangars. The English and Italians needed time for shakedown flights and repairs, so the Baltimore Flying Club came to the rescue by putting up canvas tents on the boardwalk. The American teams, one from the army, the other from the navy, arrived last, with nonchalant swagger. The navy team had set a speed record of 189 miles per hour the year before, and the army had brought in a ringer.

James H. "Jimmy" Doolittle had earned a doctorate in aeronautical engineering from MIT that June and had logged thousands of hours in the air.

The navy also flew in the pride of its seaplane fleet to put on an air show the day of the race. Twenty-three Curtiss torpedo bombers glided in and anchored offshore, while the racers put their planes through navigation and seaworthiness trials. The British team immediately ran into trouble. A pilot, who had broken his wrist playing deck tennis on the cruise over from Southampton, lost control of his daring new single-wing Supermarine S-4 and pancaked into the bay. The British support boat's motor conked out, but a teammate taxied his plane over and picked the pilot off the back of his fuselage.

That night, gale force winds blew into Bay Shore, knocking down hangars, damaging planes, and postponing the race. Worse, seventeen navy torpedo bombers had torn loose and smashed themselves to pieces on shore. Army general William "Billy" Mitchell, already in trouble for criticizing the navy after its airship *Shenandoah* crashed that September, called the loss "staggering" and blasted navy mismanagement.

On Monday, October 26, after a day of repairs, five thousand spectators rode down the "Red Rocket" line to see the great race. Unable to start his engine, one Italian pilot trudged into his hangar, ducked behind a large flower arrangement sent by Baltimore's Italian community, and cried. A British pilot broke a strut and watched helplessly as his plane's nose dipped and the propeller sawed through his pontoons. Doolittle managed to get airborne first in a dash of spray, and his army black-and-gold Curtiss biplane zoomed around the first lap at 223 miles an hour.

The navy was hot on his heels, followed by the British and Italians, but Doolittle knew how to bank into tight turns and fly low into a headwind. The navy's hopes ended when one plane's engine quit a lap short of the finish line, and the other's engine caught fire. Both pilots landed safely and watched Doolittle soar high overhead in a victory celebration.

No one knew it at the time, but the Schneider Cup race of 1925 was a bit of aeronautic history. Billy Mitchell would be court-martialed for insubordination a month later and become the subject of a Hollywood film. Benito Mussolini put Italian government money behind his racers, who dominated the Schneider Cup in the 1930s. "Jimmy" Doolittle went on to lead an air raid over Tokyo in retribution for Pearl Harbor. Most importantly, the designer of the British Supermarine plane that had pancaked into the bay found in his failure the seeds of the legendary British Spitfires that turned the Battle of Britain. And to think—for one glorious, daring, comical, sparkling moment—they were all a part of your Maryland.

Source: Michael Gough, "Doolittle Wins in Baltimore," *Airpower*, November 2005

62

CAB AND THURGOOD

In 1883, as racial segregation closed in on the nation, Baltimore converted its old German-American elementary school into the Colored High and Training School, the city's first public high school for black students. It was a two-story building with sixteen rooms. Nearly four decades later, it still would have no library, cafeteria, or gym, but that mattered little to two extraordinary young men who were about to enter its ninth grade.

One was the son of a middle-class family. His father was a railroad waiter, and his mother struggled against the powers-that-be to get teaching jobs. He was tall, slender, and light-skinned, with wavy hair and a lanky stride. The girls found him attractive. He liked to cut up as the class clown, to throw chalk and get into trouble. But he was smart. Once, the principal punished him by sending him down to the boiler room with instructions to memorize the United States Constitution before he came out. He did. He also held his own in arguments with his often angry, inebriated father. In fact, he seemed to thrive on those fights. He loved schoolwork, and that freshman year he became captain of the school's champion debating team.

The other young man knew a different side of Baltimore's streets. He had grown up poor and early on learned how to hustle. In high school, he had little use for books. Better to make money. He skipped school to wait tables, shine shoes, hawk newspapers, or "walk hots" at Pimlico. His older sister was a cabaret singer, and before long he knew the local gamblers, musicians, club owners, and numbers runners. One of his jobs was to approach soldiers home on leave and lure them into the cabaret where his sister was singing.

The Colored High and Training School was just across the street from the district police station, and from their school windows both young men could watch as suspects, many of them black, were brought in by the all-white police force. Sometimes they could even hear the interrogations, as police used brass knuckles or clubs to loosen a confession. "We could hear police in there beating the hell out of people," one said. Sometimes teachers would have to pull down the shades so the students could concentrate.

In 1925 the champion debater graduated. The class cutup and bad boy had taken "Latin, history, trigonometry, and physics, as well as machine work and wood trimming." Surprisingly, he had never once been late and had missed only a single day in four years. He had managed a B average, not as good as his older brother, who had gone on to medical school. But his mother, who pushed the boys on such things, thought he might be good enough to become a dentist . . . or maybe a lawyer.

The twentieth century has been called the American Century, and rightly so. The nation built itself into a world power and began correcting serious problems in American society. No one knew that, of course, when the class clown turned would-be lawyer marched down the aisle to his graduation. He had no money and no idea if he could even get to college, let alone law school.

As he walked down that aisle, eyes twinkling with mischief and pride, no one could have guessed that Thurgood Marshall would go on to change America as few men ever would, shattering segregation in the schools and becoming the first African American to sit on the United States Supreme Court.

But what about that other kid . . . the hustler? As it happened he turned out to be the star of that graduation ceremony. His record wasn't anything like that of his pal Thurgood Marshall, but he did put some of that streetwise musical ability to good use by singing an unforgettable rendition of a popular song—"To a Wild Rose." People talked about it for years. Later he went on to write "Minnie the Moocher." America would long remember Cab Calloway, too.

Source: Juan Williams, *Thurgood Marshall: American Revolutionary* (New York: Three Rivers Press, 1998)

▦ 63 ▦

WALLIS

er father was a young aristocrat from the Warfield family. Just before he died of tuberculosis, he named his infant daughter after eminent Baltimore attorney Severn Teackle Wallis. In straitened circumstances, Warfield's widow had to move into her mother-in-law's mansion in Baltimore and accept handouts to make ends meet. Young Wallis lived her childhood between poverty and riches, hobnobbing with prominent financiers, lawyers, and politicians, even though her mother had to make all her clothes. When the time came to send her off to boarding school, not everyone liked her. Some thought she was lively and kind, and praised the fact that despite her deep blue eyes and obvious charm, she never moved in on another girl's beau. Fondly, they called her "Skinny," a nickname she loved. Others weren't so kind. She was a climber, they said, so ambitious she'd "step on her grandmother's stomach" to get where she wanted to go.

The year she was to make her social debut at cotillion happened to be 1914, and her wealthy uncle thought it would be unseemly to throw the obligatory party with a war going on in Europe. Her godmother, one of the wealthiest women in Baltimore, did give a party—but for another girl. At the last minute, her mother's Virginia cousin, who had married the commandant of the Marine Corps, came to Wallis's rescue with a grand party in Washington. Handsome young officers in dress uniform whirled her society friends about the dance floor to the music of the full sixty-piece Marine Corps band. Glorious as the evening was, it wasn't in Baltimore, and it didn't get her into Baltimore society.

The next year, having accepted an invitation from another of her mother's cousins to visit Florida, she fell in love with a dashing young flier at the Pensacola Naval Air Station. Against the family's wishes, they married, a decision she came to regret. The dashing pilot turned out to be a jealous, abusive drunk who locked her in the bedroom and once spread all her family photographs on the floor in front of her and stepped on them. In California, where they moved following a transfer, she left him. A brief reunion in Washington after the war ended badly, and she horrified her family by filing for divorce.

There followed years of travel—to Paris with money from family, to China as a guest of friends. Along the way, there were flings, flirtations, and romantic liaisons, all conducted on the fringe of the best society. "She was always asking friends to get her invited to this party or that," one young heiress recalled. "She was *pushy*. She had to be, . . . because she was . . . never quite *in*. . . . Too many men around her, not top-drawer men, either."

Eventually, she settled in a humble hotel room in Warrenton, Virginia, where, a friend remembered her as being "only moderately attractive. Her mouth was too big, her nose was too long, and her clenched teeth grin was almost grotesque. But her eyes and her hair were very nice, so was her voice; and her figure was trim. . . . [and] She *shone* at parties! She could dance up a storm and match drinks with anyone."

Living on her husband's military allotment of $225 a month, she had to play poker—and win—for extra cash. When one Virginia gentleman proposed, she replied, "Uh-uh! . . . You're poor, and I'm poor, and we both need money."

With that uppermost in her mind, she went to New York to visit friends. There she met a young shipping magnate who was divorcing his wife. He was mild-tempered, intelligent, and even better, wealthy. Yet when he asked her to marry him and move to London, she refused. One friend said it was because, at thirty-one and destitute, she needed time to check his financial status. From France, where she had gone again to stay with friends, she wrote to tell him that she had reconsidered and would marry him if he gave her a Buick convertible and a month-long tour of the Continent. He agreed. Happy at last, she told a friend, "I'll never have to sing for my supper anymore. I'm going to live in England and have a little garden and lead a quiet life. Nobody will ever see or hear of me again!" Her friend laughed and joked, "Don't fall in love with the Prince of Wales."

No one could see it at the time, but the course of European history was about to change.

Source: J. Bryan III and Charles J. V. Murphy, *The Windsor Story* (New York: William Morrow, 1979)

64

HATRACK

In April 1926, good and evil met head to head in Boston at a place aptly named "Brimstone Corner." Representing morality, propriety, and social order was the Boston Watch and Ward Society and its redoubtable leader, J. Franklin Chase. Rising to confront them from the depths of Jazz Age, Prohibition-hating Baltimore, came that blue-eyed devil himself, H. L. Mencken. The fracas had begun when Mencken's *American Mercury* published a short story by Herbert Asbury titled, "Hatrack." It was a none-too-subtle attack on religious hypocrisy. In the story, Hatrack, a good-hearted small-town prostitute, goes to church every Sunday evening in search of respectability. And every Sunday evening, the congregation scorns and rebukes her. Then, Monday through Saturday, the churchmen buy her services.

Chase and the Watch and Ward had long had it in for Mencken, whom they regarded as the Antichrist, and for them "Hatrack" was the last straw. As for Mencken, he had once remarked that Puritans like Chase were haunted by the fear that someone, somewhere, might be happy. When the Watch and Ward Society banned the sale of his magazine in Boston, Mencken fired off letters to newspaper editors across the country, announcing his intention to make "Hatrack" a test case of censorship. On April 4, simmering with rage, he boarded a train for Boston.

The next morning, with a bundle of *American Mercury*s under his arm, he made his way to "Brimstone Corner" in the company of attorney Arthur Garfield Hays, lately of the Scopes Trial in Tennessee. In front of the Park Street Church, they encountered hundreds of Harvard students, all ardent fans of the *Mercury*, and all eager to glimpse their hero.

In a few minutes, J. Franklin Chase and some plainclothes policemen showed up. The two men glared at one another. Chase asked Mencken if he would sell him a copy of the April issue of the magazine. Mencken politely replied that he would. Chase handed him a fifty-cent piece. Mencken's eyes lit up. With a wink to the students, he bit it to test its authenticity. Amid the howls of laughter, he handed Chase a copy of the *Mercury*. Chase pointed a quivering finger and shouted, "Arrest that man!" As the police led Mencken away, he threw his bundle of magazines in the air, creating pandemonium in the crowd of souvenir-hunting students. Then, arm in arm with the cops, he walked the four blocks to the courthouse and a hearing before a magistrate who might very well send him to jail.

The Watch and Ward Society's attorney handed the judge a red underlined copy of "Hatrack," denouncing it as obscene. Mencken, who was looking at a year or two in the slammer, replied that he was indeed the editor of the magazine, and he took full responsibility for its contents. Arthur Garfield Hays intoned that this was a grave matter of constitutional importance. The judge, who happened to be a Unitarian and a liberal thinker, then took the magazine home with him to read before making a decision. "It's a cinch," one reporter said. "Chase always wins." But the next day the judge announced that he could find no offense in "Hatrack" and dismissed the case.

In triumph, Mencken marched off to Harvard's Union Hall, where two thousand students who had just learned of his court triumph crowded to see him. Professor Felix Frankfurter, a noted defender of civil liberties, said that Mencken had done a "dreadful and brave thing. His was the courage to resist brutality." Mencken acknowledged the cheers, then unfurled a large Maryland flag. "I want to give you something that I know you will appreciate, thinking as you do," he told the students. "This is the flag of the Free State of Maryland, of which I have the honor to be a citizen." He added, "The best thing about liberty is that it is such a charming thing to fight for."

The April issue of the *American Mercury* quickly sold out in Boston, as elsewhere, and the last copy was stolen from the public library. For a brief moment, Puritanism and censorship had been defeated. Mencken was at the height of his power. "The *American Mercury* was our Bible," one Harvard student gushed, "and Mencken was our god."

Sources: Marion Elizabeth Rodgers, *Mencken, the American Iconoclast: The Life and Times of the Bad Boy of Baltimore* (New York: Oxford University Press, 2005); Fred Hobson, *Mencken: A Life* (New York: Random House, 1994); Terry Teachout, *The Skeptic: A Life of H. L. Mencken* (New York: HarperCollins, 2002)

⬚ 65 ⬚

THE CRACK-UP

Nineteen thirty-two was a difficult year for Scott and Zelda Fitzgerald. Since their first trip to Europe in the summer of 1921, they'd spent much of their time traveling in France, Italy, and Switzerland. But in 1930, Zelda had suffered a nervous breakdown. In February of 1932, following the death of her father, she suffered another. The Fitzgeralds came to Baltimore so she could be admitted for psychiatric treatment at the Phipps Clinic of the Johns Hopkins Hospital, where she would remain until June.

While Zelda was undergoing treatment, Scott rented a large Victorian mansion, La Paix, and moved in with their ten-year-old daughter, Frances. There, amid the trees on what is now the grounds of St. Joseph's Hospital in Towson, he worried about his career. A decade earlier he'd burst upon the American literary landscape in a blaze of glory. *This Side of Paradise*, *The Beautiful and the Damned*, *Tales of the Jazz Age*, and *The Great Gatsby* had made him a highly regarded novelist and a popular literary celebrity. Drinking and socializing their way through Europe with the likes of Ernest Hemingway, Ring Lardner, and John Dos Passos, Scott and Zelda Fitzgerald became cultural icons, embodying the glamour and dizzy energy of the Jazz Age.

But these were darker days. Years of European travel and lavish living had drained Fitzgerald financially, and as the hard years of the Great Depression gripped the country, he began to worry that his writing, too, was in decline. To dull the fear, he drank—hard. In *A Moveable Feast*, Hemingway described one evening they'd spent together in Paris. "As he sat there at the bar holding the glass of champagne, the skin seemed to tighten over his face," Hemingway wrote, "and then it drew tighter until the face was like a death's head." Hemingway later told editor Maxwell Perkins, "Scott died inside himself around the age of thirty to thirty-five, and his creative powers died somewhat later." Apparently Hemingway was right, because when *Tender Is the Night*—the book Fitzgerald was working on at La Paix—appeared in 1934, it was a critical and commercial disaster.

Making matters worse was Zelda's illness. Her impulsiveness and severe mood swings may have indicated bipolar disorder. A Towson newspaper even suggested schizophrenia. Scott was later to comment that all his hopes and optimism for the future were left behind on the little country roads leading up to the sanitariums that Zelda had visited in Europe. Perhaps significantly, he did not say Baltimore.

There are those who suggest that Zelda was jealous of Scott's talent as a writer, that she encouraged him to drink and waste himself. In October 1932, a few months after she was discharged from Phipps, Zelda published her own novel, *Save Me the Waltz*. Scott, of course, read it and angrily accused her of stealing material from *Tender Is the Night*. A year later, when a fire broke out that destroyed much of La Paix, an ugly rumor circulated that Zelda herself had set it.

In December of 1933, Scott found them an apartment at 1307 Park Avenue in Baltimore. The next month Zelda had a third nervous breakdown and was admitted to Sheppard Pratt for treatment. A series of hospitals in New York and North Carolina followed.

As Zelda went to North Carolina, Scott, too, went south, then west to Hollywood to work on a faltering career as a screenwriter. Their time in Baltimore had been a brief, if hardly peaceful sojourn in two tumultuous lives, but it would also be the last time they really lived together. Scott died of a heart attack on December 21, 1940. Zelda died in North Carolina in March of 1948, trapped in a hospital fire. She was buried with Scott in Rockville.

Like a flash of sunlight on a brilliant yellow roadster, Scott and Zelda Fitzgerald's fame burned bright and fast, and then they were gone. The Jazz Age was over.

Source: Material provided by Donna B. Shear

66

KING KONG

This is the story of a man, a woman, and a movie. The man was Merian C. Cooper, a 1915 graduate of the Naval Academy and a guy who liked to live on the edge. In 1916 he went off to chase Pancho Villa with the Georgia National Guard. Then he joined the new army air corps as a bomber pilot in World War I and was shot down in flames over Germany in September 1918. The Armistice saw him recovering in a German hospital, but no sooner was he released than he volunteered to help Poland fight off an invasion by the new Soviet Red Army. He recruited fifteen other American pilots and four Poles and formed the Kosciusko Squadron. They shot up the Bolsheviks so badly, the Russians put a bounty on Cooper's head.

The woman was Marguerite Harrison, the daughter of a shipping magnate, who had grown up in Catonsville, attended the best schools, and married a stockbroker. When her husband died broke, she took a job as a reporter for the *Baltimore Sun*. She, too, loved adventure and wanted to see Europe after the war. With the newspaper's permission and the blessing of Military Intelligence, she traveled to Germany, dodged gunfire in the streets of Berlin, and sent back reports on the increasing social and political chaos. In search of ever more excitement, she lobbied to get into Russia for a firsthand look at the Revolution.

Undaunted by official resistance, she traveled on her own to Warsaw and took a room at the Bristol Hotel. There, at a ball, she met and danced away the night with a handsome American pilot, named Merian Cooper.

Cooper went back to the front, was again shot down, and was thrown into a Russian prison at Belyov. To keep from being executed—remember, he had a price on his head—he adopted the name of Frank Mosher. Harrison also made her way into Russia, accompanied by another woman. In a few weeks an American turncoat informed the Russians that Harrison was sending reports back to the American government. The secret police kept an eye on her but let her continue. When she got word of a captured American, Frank Mosher, she sent him packages of food through the Red Cross with her name attached. Back came a note penciled on a cigarette wrapper: "My name is not Mosher. I am Merian C. Cooper. . . . Don't you remember dancing with me at the ball in the Hotel Bristol in Warsaw?" Shortly thereafter, she was arrested and tossed into the dreaded Lubianka prison.

Fortunately, both of them got out of Russia. Cooper, naturally, made a daring escape from a forest prison camp. Then a Maryland senator intervened and secured Marguerite's release. When she got back to Berlin, Cooper was there to greet her and tell her that those packages of food had saved his life.

In 1923, Cooper conceived the idea of making a documentary about a tribe of nomads in western Persia. When Marguerite found out about it, she put up half the money for the expedition on condition that she could go along. She, Cooper, and cameraman Ernest Schoedsack set out to film the trek of a band of nomads forced to leave their drought-stricken land in western Persia and move east across rugged terrain to better pastures. Schoedsack took an immediate dislike to Marguerite, who wanted to appear in the film, insisted on putting on makeup before every shot, and treated the whole thing like a family outing in Catonsville. Still, she was right there when the tribe crossed the swift and dangerous Karun River on make-shift floats, then climbed barefoot over a fifteen-thousand-foot, snow-covered mountain. When they reached their promised land, Cooper and Schoedsack had a powerful documentary, *Grass: A Nation's Battle for Life.*

Harrison and Cooper then went their separate ways, she to marry and live out her life in Baltimore, he to Hollywood to make more movies. In 1933 he made one about an expedition to a dangerous island. Schoedsack's wife, who wrote the script, remembered her husband's disdain for Marguerite in *Grass* and included a part for an "unwanted woman." Cooper convinced Fay Wray to take the role by telling her she'd have the "tallest, darkest leading man" in Hollywood as a co-star. Did she ever. You probably didn't know it, but King Kong, that big ape who climbed the Empire State Building, owed a little something to your Maryland.

Source: Wallace Shugg, "The Socialite Spy from Baltimore: Marguerite E. Harrison, 1918–1922," unpublished manuscript, provided by the author

❈ 67 ❈

OMAHA BEACH

An hour past dawn, on June 6, 1944, ten miles off the coast of Normandy, the first two hundred US landing craft left the largest invasion fleet ever assembled and headed for a place called Omaha Beach. The men had already been in the open boats for four hours. They had watched huge battleships pulverize the German defenses, and waves of bombers had roared over their heads to destroy whatever the navy had missed. But nothing the ships and planes did could cheer the landing force. Cold, wet, and seasick, all they wanted to do was get out of those boats.

They had never seen a battle before, but their officers told them that the landing would be unopposed. That was untrue. Waiting for them on the bluffs above Omaha was the tough German 352nd Division, in bunkers that could withstand the biggest shells the navy had. And most of those shells had missed. Heavy clouds had also forced the bombers to drop their loads far inland.

At low tide, 5:25 that morning, the gold sand beach was between four and five hundred meters wide. Land mines numbered in the hundreds of thousands. As the barrage lifted, the German gunners went to battle stations. Their machine guns, mortars, and artillery were aimed out to sea and up and down the beach. The Americans would be in their sights a long time before they reached the bluffs, and under a terrible crossfire.

Meticulous and efficient, the Germans had charts in the gun positions showing beach landmarks and the range to each.

A navy beach master, whose job was to mark a path through the obstacles for the landing craft, was in the first boat to hit the beach that awful morning. He later remembered looking up at the Germans in plain sight on the bluff above and wondering why they didn't shoot him. He did not know that across the bluffs telephones were at that moment chattering with the order: Wait until the Americans reach the waterline. Moments later, the first wave of little wooden Higgins boats roared in among the obstacles and dropped their ramps. Above them, the enemy squinted into their gunsights, and the battle for Omaha Beach began.

"It's not like in Hollywood," one veteran bitterly recalled. "The actors jump into the water and in three seconds they're charging up the beach. Well, it isn't like that." Just before they ran aground on the sand, his captain called out, "It's an unopposed landing!" But bullets hit the boat just as its ramp went down. "The first few minutes in the water, I will never forget as long as I live," he said. "There were machine guns, rifle fire, mortar fire, 88s and God knows what else. And it felt as though every German was aiming at me." Landing craft began to stack up behind one another. Men carrying eighty pounds of equipment jumped off into deeper water. Sometimes it took half an hour to wade ashore. The only cover was hundreds of yards away. And that "cover," a low ridge of smooth stones called the "shingle," was a trap under the eyes of waiting German mortar crews.

It's almost a miracle that anyone got off Omaha Beach alive. Everything that could go wrong did. The men had been on the boats too long and had to carry too much equipment. Many drowned unnecessarily. Landing craft came in at the wrong places, and in clusters, making them easy targets for an enemy who was very good at what they did.

And yet, after hours of suffering the worst trials men could endure, they decided they had had enough. Alone and in small groups, they crossed the shingle and the sea wall, worked their way through the mines and up the steep bluffs and one by one put the bunkers and pillboxes out of action. By noon, Omaha Beach was theirs. They were from Maryland, Virginia, and Pennsylvania, and they were known as the Twenty-Ninth or "Blue and Gray" Division—the "Twenty-Niners." And no men, anywhere, have ever fought a battle more impossible than the one they fought, on the morning of June 6, 1944, on Omaha Beach.

Source: Quotes and material from Stephen E. Ambrose, *D-Day, June 6, 1944: The Climactic Battle of World War II* (New York: Simon and Schuster, 1994)

▣ 68 ▣

CANAJOHARIE AT THE GUT

The winter of 1944 came in as the coldest Northern Europe had seen in forty years. American GIs fighting their way across France and Belgium shivered in lightweight summer uniforms and often went without hot food. As Christmas approached that bitter December, a lone squad of the US Twenty-Ninth Division came upon a German manor house on the west side of the Roer River, just inside the German border. Approaching a farmhouse from the front could be suicidal, but they had orders to take and hold it. Warily they started forward, but the only occupants turned out to be an old woman and a terrified German soldier who was more than ready to surrender.

Another pleasant surprise awaited them. The cellar was packed with food—flour, sugar, apples, vintage cider, milk cans filled with cooked meat, and preserved eggs. Cattle grazed nearby. Chickens cackled in their pens. A cart filled with potatoes sat outside. One of the men made breakfast. Soon the hungry squad was looking at eggs sunny-side up, pancakes dripping with syrup made from sugar and cinnamon, apple cider, and coffee. A slender, pimply-faced boy, nicknamed "Canajoharie" after his hometown in New York, found a motorcycle leaning against the house and tinkered with it until he got it running.

The rest of the squad gathered to watch him ride in tight circles around the yard. The German word for the farm was

"Das Gut." And so they spent that Christmas at "the Gut," warm, comfortable, safe, and laughing at Canajoharie and his motorcycle.

The Battle of the Bulge erupted thirty miles to the south, and the squad went back to the fighting. They returned to the west bank of the Roer a few weeks later, banged up, some wounded, and took a position in another deserted house. German soldiers watched them from across the river, but both sides were tired and soon reached a mutual understanding on how they would conduct the war. Headquarters wanted action and sent a daily allotment of mortar shells. The Americans dutifully lobbed theirs across the river every day at noon. The Germans replied with a small barrage at dusk. No one was hurt, and headquarters was satisfied.

Then, early one morning, the Americans awoke to the roar of a motorcycle coming from the German side. After making sure they were awake, it calmly putted down the road at a stately pace. The GIs concluded it must be a dispatch rider. The next morning, the motorcycle roared again. Angrily, the Twenty-Niners fired off their mortar shells. The Germans immediately retaliated. The Americans spent the rest of the day thinking how they could put an end to the dispatch rider, and they called for more shells, which headquarters happily supplied. Using every map and reconnaissance report they could find, they plotted his route along the road behind the German lines and set up pre-aligned aiming stakes so their mortar could track him on his ride.

The next morning at dawn, they were in the mortar pit, waiting... listening. Across the river, the dispatch rider kicked his motorcycle to life and gunned the throttle. The Americans fired the first of their shells high in the air. Unaware of what was about to befall him, the motorcyclist began his run, put-putting down the road.

Before the first shells had landed, the GIs shifted their mortar to a second position and fired, then a third. The German guns thundered back, driving them into the farmhouse cellar, but between explosions they clearly heard the dispatch rider and his motorcycle safely put-put-putting off into the distance.

The Twenty-Niners were furious. That dispatch rider was spitting in their eye. They radioed headquarters for more shells and were making new plans for the next morning when their old sergeant cleared his throat. Thinking back to that warm and peaceful Christmas, he said quietly, "Reminds me of Canajoharie at the Gut."

The next morning, the motorcycle defiantly coughed and growled again, but this time the Twenty-Niners paid no attention, except for the one who told this story years later. He thought back to Christmas, too, and wished that unknown rider Godspeed.

Source: Emil Willimetz, "From Normandy to the Roer: A Footsoldier's Unsentimental Account of Combat with the 29th Division," *Maryland Historical Magazine* 96 (2001): 185–220

▩ 69 ▩

TUNNEL JOE

O n Monday, February 19, 1951, Baltimore newspaper headlines announced that thirty-nine-year-old Joseph E.
Holmes had escaped from the Maryland State Penitentiary.
Holmes was already notorious as "the dinner-
time burglar" who liked to rob houses in
well-to-do neighborhoods while families
were gathered around the dinner table.

But what made readers shake
their heads in wonder was the astonishing way Holmes had gotten
out. Apparently, he had cut his
way through two inches of slate
and ten inches of concrete in the
floor of his cell without anybody
being the wiser. Then he'd dug a
seventy-foot tunnel through the earth
and clay under the prison's massive
stone wall—a tunnel that hadn't collapsed—and popped up onto the grassy
plot along Eager Street. After easily climbing
the seven-foot iron fence, he'd vanished into the night.

The only inmate ever to tunnel his way out of Maryland's
maximum-security prison became an instant celebrity. People

began calling him "Tunnel Joe." "It's the most fantastic escape I've ever heard of," said the warden. "That guy must have been an engineer."

Tunnel Joe wasn't an engineer, but he was ingenious. For a year he'd concealed his work by flushing enormous amounts of dirt down the toilet in his cell while remaining immaculately clean himself. "I perceive great possibilities in this man," said Eugene O'Dunne, a former Baltimore City judge who had investigated corruption at the pen forty years earlier.

One fellow thought Holmes should be sent to Washington to lead a Senate investigating committee. "Mr. Holmes has demonstrated, with tremendous success, his abilities as a prober. He is one man who can justifiably claim to have really reached the bottom of things." Another called him "just the man to solve the problem of constructing a tunnel under Baltimore harbor."

By that time Joe was in Philadelphia looking for a job, but he thought he first needed a Social Security card and realized he didn't have one. "I was a fool," he said later, "You can't get anywhere these days without a Social Security card." He was wrong about that, and it cost him. Discouraged, he returned to Baltimore.

On Saturday, March 3, a few minutes before eight o'clock, a man in a brown coat and fawn hat accosted sixty-four-year-old Mary Ruiz at the base of the Washington Monument. He pointed a gun at her, took her pocketbook containing five dollars, and disappeared. She ran to a nearby store and reported the holdup.

Minutes later, Officer Frank Plunkett spotted a man at Monument and Cathedral Streets fitting the robber's description. When he got out of his radio car and grabbed the suspect by the arm, the man shoved a .32 caliber revolver into his stomach and pulled the trigger. The gun misfired—twice—and the robber fled. Plunkett and two other policemen chased the suspect through the Saturday night crowds in Mt. Vernon and into the Recreational Bowling Alley at Howard and Monument. There they cornered him. One shouted "Hey, you're Holmes!"

"Yes," Joe said.

Before he was sentenced to another thirty years in the penitentiary, Joe told what everyone wanted to know—how he had dug the tunnel. Prison officials as far away as California wanted their guards to know, so it wouldn't happen to them.

Joe told them every detail, then he explained why he'd done it. Apparently, a new warden had decided to tighten discipline at the penitentiary. One of his "reforms" had been to take away inmates' ability to earn a little money by making and selling knick-knacks. "I had no future to look forward to," Joe said. He thought he might "blow his top" if he didn't get out.

He also described what it had felt like, when, after working eleven months on that tunnel, digging seventy feet under the dark, heavy prison walls, he had finally been able to open a tiny hole just outside with his fingers. He said he looked up to see a clear, cold night sky filled with stars. "That," he said, "gave me a deal of satisfaction."

Joseph Ellsworth Holmes, inmate #32565, became a hero to the African American community in Maryland, the subject of a song, and a local legend. We can only wonder what he might have accomplished in life had he gotten that Social Security card.

Source: Wallace Shugg, *A Monument to Good Intentions: The Story of the Maryland Penitentiary, 1804–1995* (Baltimore: Maryland Historical Society, 2000)

▨ 70 ▨

JOHNNY U.

From the beginning, coaches believed that boys from de-prived childhoods made the best football players—like the kid growing up in Pittsburgh, who lost his father when he was five. His mother took over the family coal business, and he delivered coal into his neighbors' cellars, shoveling two tons for a quarter. But he hardly grew. As a high school quarter-back, he stood five-foot-ten and weighed only 135 pounds. He was unbearably shy. On Friday nights, he'd take his girl and her girlfriend to the school dance, then wait for them in the parking lot until it was over.

He made All-City quarterback his senior year, but no one cared. Notre Dame thought he was too small to play, that he'd get hurt. Indiana was interested for a while, then changed its mind. He went to Louisville and earned the starter's job his freshman year. Two years later the team plunged to medioc-rity in an academic scandal, and any buzz among the pro scouts all but vanished. The Pittsburgh Steelers eventually took him in the ninth round of the draft.

When he reported to camp in the summer of 1955, the Pittsburgh veterans began calling him "Clem" after comedian Red Skelton's character, Clem Kadiddlehopper. When he asked for his daily whites—the t-shirt, shorts, socks, and ath-letic supporter stacked at every player's locker—the trainer pointed to a pile on the floor and told him to pick them out himself. The coach didn't like him either. The Steelers already had three quarterbacks, and the kid was slow to learn the playbook. Through five exhibition games, he didn't take a snap. The owner's sons were amazed by his accuracy throwing the ball in practice and pleaded with their father to give him a shot, but three weeks before the season started, he was cut. He hitchhiked home to save bus fare. His young wife—the girl he'd waited for in the parking lot—met him at the door with a present. She had bought tickets so their families could see him at the Steelers' home opener.

The Cleveland Browns needed help at quarterback but at the last minute coaxed the legendary Otto Graham out of retirement. Maybe next year, they said. The kid started working construction and playing semipro ball for six dollars a game in the Steel Bowl Conference. He told his wife to take the six dollars and not pay bills but do something for herself.

Down in Baltimore, the Colts were rebuilding under Coach Weeb Eubank, becoming younger, bigger, faster, better. One day Eubank got an unsigned postcard from Pittsburgh. "There's a boy in sandlot ball here, . . . who's worth looking at," it said. Eubank already had a quarterback in George Shaw, but when his backup retired to attend law school, Eubank gave the kid a call.

Baltimore, the kid discovered, was nothing like Pittsburgh. His daily whites were piled neatly by his locker. Veterans took him aside and taught him things. The spirit was infectious. Eubank worked on his passing. Thinking the kid threw too low, he strung a volleyball net across the line of scrimmage and had him throw everything over it.

In the fourth game of the season, against the Chicago Bears, Shaw went down with an injury. The kid took over at quarterback and became an instant disaster. He fumbled his first handoff, leading to a Bears touchdown. Chicago intercepted his first pass and ran it all the way back for another. The final humiliating score was Bears 58, Colts 27. Nevertheless, he impressed teammates and opponents alike with his toughness, his willingness to stand in until the last minute before getting rid of the ball. The next week, he led the Colts to a 28–21 win over the Packers. In New York, as he trotted onto the field, still undersized and bony, with painfully skinny legs, Giants quarterback Charlie Conerly turned to star running back Frank Gifford and said, "Look at that goofy s.o.b." Gifford and Conerly didn't know it, but they, and the rest of pro football, were about to meet Johnny Unitas, the greatest quarterback ever to play the game.

Source: Michael MacCambridge, *America's Game: The Epic Story of How Pro Football Captured a Nation* (New York: Random House, 2004)

71

THE GREATEST FOOTBALL
GAME EVER PLAYED

In 1958 the New York Giants were the class of the National Football League. They'd lost all five exhibition games at the beginning of the season, but no one counted them out, not with the likes of Roosevelt Grier, Andy Robustelli, Kyle Rote, and Alex Webster. Rugged West Virginia middle linebacker Sam Huff anchored the league's best defense. Marine veteran Charlie Conerly handed off to Frank Gifford, a versatile halfback and Hollywood film extra who'd appeared in a James Garner war movie. As the Giants marched through the season, it soon became clear that their stiffest opposition would come from an upstart outfit in Baltimore.

The Colts finished atop the Western Conference by a wide margin. Not so the Giants, who had to win the Eastern Conference by first beating the Cleveland Browns and their fearsome running back, Jim Brown. Linebacker Huff had already lost his front teeth to a collision with Brown, but in the Conference final Tom Landry's New York defense held Brown to just eight yards, and the Giants won 10–0.

The NFL championship was played on December 28 before a less than sell-out crowd in Yankee Stadium. Under a steel gray winter sky, banged up and bruised after the battle in

Cleveland, the Giants looked across the field at their old adversaries in blue and white. They'd lost to those horseshoes twice in exhibition play, but had beaten Baltimore 24–21 in the regular season.

Still, they knew what to expect from the likes of Donovan, Pellington, Berry, Moore, Ameche, and a quarterback Conerly once called "that goofy looking s.o.b." Johnny Unitas, two years removed from being a Pittsburgh Steeler washout, was recovering from a punctured lung, but by now the Giants knew how tough he really was.

The first half of the game was a mix of ugliness and football brilliance. New York scored first on a field goal. The proud Giant defense ripped the Colt line time and again to harass and sack Unitas. But twice the Colt lightning struck. At halftime, the score was 14–3 Colts, who looked better than the three-and-a-half point favorites they were.

In the second half, Baltimore barely missed a third touchdown after Alan Ameche mixed up his signals. New York struck back. Mel Triplett ran for a touchdown, then Gifford, to give New York a 17–14 lead. Linebacker Huff hit Berry out of bounds and exchanged punches with Baltimore coach Weeb Eubank. As the clock ran down, New York again got the ball on their nineteen. On third and four from the Giants forty, Gifford hurled himself off right tackle but was met by Colt defensive end Gino Marchetti, followed by Big Daddy Lipscomb, whose hit broke Marchetti's ankle in two places. As they carried Marchetti off the field, officials placed the ball a foot short of the first down the Giants needed to run out the clock. On the sidelines, Gifford raged as his team punted. But the football now belonged to John Constantine Unitas.

"We got 86 yards and two minutes," Unitas told his offense. "Let's get to work." Marchetti, on a stretcher, told the six men carrying him that he wasn't going to the locker room just yet. Seven plays—three of them precision passes to Raymond Berry, with whom he practiced timing patterns late into winter afternoons—and Unitas had the Colts in field-goal range. Moments later, the score was tied 17–17. Time ran out. Seconds after that, millions of television screens across the nation went black. Baltimore fans surging toward the field had kicked loose a cable connection.

On the Giants' bench, a puzzled Pat Summerall asked Kyle Rote, "What happens now?"

"I guess," said Rote, "we play some more."

The Colts lost the sudden-death coin toss, kicked off, and promptly stopped the Giant offense. Cool as a riverboat gambler, Unitas trotted back onto the field and called the now-famous "Thirteen Plays," eleven of which were missed by the entire country. Just before the television picture returned, Unitas fired a pass between Huff's arm and his helmet's ear hole that found Raymond Berry at the Giants' eight. Two plays later, Alan "The Horse" Ameche plunged over from the one-yard line. Final score: Colts 23, Giants 17. What has come to be called the greatest football game ever played was history.

Sources: Frank Gifford and Harry Waters, *The Whole Ten Yards* (New York: Random House, 1993); Michael MacCambridge, *America's Game: The Epic Story of How Pro Football Captured a Nation* (New York: Random House, 2004); John F. Steadman, *The Greatest Football Game Ever Played: When the Baltimore Colts and the New York Giants Faced Sudden Death* (Baltimore: Press Box, 1988)

▪72▪

SILENT SPRING

I n June 1962, the *New Yorker* published a series of three land-
mark articles that shook Americans' faith in progress. They
were taken from a book written by a petite, attractive woman
in her mid-fifties, who resided in Silver Spring. Rachel Louise
Carson had begun writing as a little girl growing up in western
Pennsylvania. After college, where she was introduced to marine biology, she came to Johns Hopkins and earned a master's
degree in marine science but ran out of money before she
could earn a doctorate. To make ends meet, she took a job at
what is now the US Fisheries and Wildlife Service, writing radio programs about marine life. In the years that followed, she
produced two best-selling books about the sea and the mirac-
ulous and beautiful forms of life in it.

As a single writer, her life seemed successful enough. Then,
in 1957, the US Department of Agriculture undertook massive
spraying operations to eradicate fire ants in the South, gypsy
moths on Long Island, and Dutch Elm disease. The chemical
agent was a new synthetic pesticide, dichlorodiphenyltrichlo-
roethane (DDT). Carson had long worried about the toxic
effects of DDT, but now she worried even more that the government used it with no one questioning its safety. The issue at
stake was more than the country's faith in the government and
the chemical industry. It was that man thought nature could
and should be conquered.

As she began reading everything available on agricultural chemicals for another book, she received the devastating news that she had developed breast cancer. Despite debilitating radiation treatments and frequent attacks of angina, she finished it, then submitted the manuscript to rigorous fact-checking, peer review, and endless revision. A relatively small Boston publishing house, Houghton Mifflin, accepted it, and settled on the title, *Silent Spring*.

The chemical industry got wind of what was coming and tried to stop it by threatening Houghton Mifflin and the *New Yorker*. Both replied that everything in the book had been thoroughly checked. "Go ahead and sue," the *New Yorker*'s legal counsel shot back. Learning that the Audubon Society might serialize it, lawyers from one company took the society's editors to lunch and hinted that it would be a shame if their families lost their financial security.

That summer of 1962, between the time the articles appeared and the book's publication in September, the industry mounted a quarter of a million dollar public relations campaign against Carson. It was effective. One letter to the *New Yorker* from San Francisco labeled Carson a communist. "We can live without birds and animals," it said, "but . . . we cannot live without business. . . . As for insects, isn't it just like a woman to be scared to death of a few little bugs? As long as we have the H-bomb everything will be O.K."

After publication, as the campaign against the book grew, Fred Friendly of CBS asked Carson if she would appear on his network's prestigious show, *CBS Reports*, with Eric Severeid. Severeid and a film crew came to Silver Spring in November. Weak and ill from cancer treatments, Carson nevertheless appeared poised and articulate, but Severeid told his producer they had to air the show quickly. "You've got a dead leading lady," he warned.

When *CBS Reports* finally aired four months later, three of its five leading sponsors had withdrawn their support, but the campaign of intimidation had also failed. US Supreme Court justice William O. Douglas pronounced *Silent Spring* "the most important chronicle of this century for the human race," another *Uncle Tom's Cabin*. And President John F. Kennedy said he would look into the careless use of pesticides.

Rachel Carson's health was rapidly failing. She would succumb to cancer only a year after appearing on *CBS Reports*. But a sea change had occurred in public opinion. Angry letters poured into editorial and government offices, asking about the dangers of agricultural chemicals. As Carson herself put it, people no longer "assumed that someone was looking after things."

Source: Linda Lear, *Rachel Carson: Witness for Nature* (New York: Henry Holt, 1997)

ACKNOWLEDGMENTS

I want to thank former colleagues at the Maryland Historical Society, notably Paul Rubenson, Leslie Humphries, Don Renaud, and the redoubtable Louise Brownell, who, when asked to read parts, gladly lent their time and their voices. Special thanks, too, to Susan Harmon, then a flutist with the Baltimore Ravens Marching Band, who interpreted the haunting music that once emerged from poet Sidney Lanier's flute in the wintery dusk to comfort the haggard, starving prisoners of Point Lookout.

Editors Patricia Anderson and Donna Shear patiently listened while I timed, rehearsed, and "buffed" those early episodes. Wally Shugg, Jack Wennersten, Tim Riordan, Fred Rasmussen, and Kathleen Sander inspired stories. At WYPR, a radio station of which Marylanders should be proud, Tony Brandon, Andy Bienstock, Paul Hollis, Bob White, Diane Finlayson, Mary Rose Madden, Marc Steiner, and Dan Rodricks have been ever cordial and supportive. About Lisa Morgan, the show's thoughtful, considerate producer and a careful listener who catches the smallest of glitches, I cannot speak highly enough. We've been a team since the show's inception, and I hope we continue the work for many more years.

I am most grateful to Catherine Goldstead, my editor at Johns Hopkins University Press, together with those who reviewed the manuscript and the editorial board that accepted it. Though I had been approached about publication before, Catherine was the first to see the wisdom of not producing the whole oeuvre at once and kindly agreed to organize the book so as to more closely emulate the radio experience. When listeners tune in, they don't know what they're going to hear. By arranging the pieces chronologically, we have given the book some small degree of organization while effectively preserving that randomness. My thanks, too, to the design and editorial staff who produced this handsome little book and to the talented Annie Howe, who enlivened it with her illustrations.

I cannot begin to repay my wife, Barbara, for all the weekends I spent writing these pieces, for her unflagging encouragement, and for patiently listening for gaps as I read her the first drafts. But we have been amply compensated with some wonderful moments sitting together in front of the radio each Thursday evening at 5:44, when "it's time for . . . *Your Maryland.*" I hope you'll join us.

ESSAY ON SOURCES

The inspiration for "Voyage of Discovery" came from Susan Schmidt's thoughtful *Landfall along the Chesapeake: In the Wake of Captain John Smith* (Baltimore: Johns Hopkins University Press, 2006). Quotes from Smith can be found in his journals, now online at www.johnsmith400.org/journal firstvoyage.htm. The Calvert family's adventure in "Avalon" is to be found in Thomas M. Coakley, "George Calvert and Newfoundland: The Sad Face of Winter," *Maryland Historical Magazine* 100 (2005): 7–28. Additional sources for Calvert family history are James W. Foster, *George Calvert: The Early Years* (Baltimore: Maryland Historical Society, 1983), and William Hand Browne, *George Calvert and Cecilius Calvert, Barons Baltimore of Baltimore* (1890), available digitally from the Library of Congress and in softcover from Amazon.com.

Some of the characters who populated the colony in its earliest days remind us that those who came here first were not all of sterling character. John Dandy, the "murderous" gunsmith of St. Mary's, comes to life courtesy of material supplied by Timothy B. Riordan, who was then chief archaeologist at Historic St. Mary's City. In addition to the unfortunate Mary Lee (see *Archives of Maryland*, 3:306–8), other women accused of witchcraft left written records. Rebecca Fowler's ordeal is recounted in Raphael Semmes, *Crime and Punishment in Early Maryland* (Baltimore: Johns Hopkins Press, 1938),

168–69; Virtue Violl's encounter with the law may be found in C. Ashley Ellefson, "William Bladen of Annapolis, 1673?–1718: 'the most capable in all Respects' or 'Blockhead Booby'?," 166, available online from the Maryland State Archives. "The Monster" drew upon several sources but mainly Lawrence C. Wroth, "The Story of Thomas Cresap, a Maryland Pioneer," *Maryland Historical Magazine* 9 (1914): 1–35. The story of Captain Louis Guillar and his frightening ship, *La Paix*, demonstrates that the rough-and-tumble of colonial life could easily turn to sheer terror. It appeared more than a century ago in Henry F. Thompson, "A Pirate on the Chesapeake," *Maryland Historical Magazine* 1 (1906): 15–27.

The men who defied the Crown in "The Summer of '76" risked the same fate as befell Guillar's pirates. Their story is drawn from Ronald Hoffman, *A Spirit of Dissension: Economics, Politics, and the Revolution in Maryland* (Baltimore: Johns Hopkins University Press, 1973). Escaping the cruelties of eighteenth-century justice, too, was Charles Willson Peale, who went on to become one of the new nation's most important artists. His story is to be found in Robert Plate, *Charles Willson Peale: Son of Liberty, Father of Art and Science* (New York: David McKay Company, 1967). For John Kilby and the band of imprisoned Chesapeake privateersmen who flaunted their defiance—to the cheers of British spectators—before taking part in a legendary naval battle, see Durwood T. Stokes, ed., "The Narrative of John Kilby," *Maryland Historical Magazine* 67 (1972): 21–33. Roger Novak's "The *Mermaid* of Assateague," *Maryland Historical Magazine* 102 (2007): 194–203, tells us of one British captain who by his actions demonstrated that the Royal Navy had its share of good-hearted gentlemen.

One spectacular light of the new republic was Baltimore's own Elizabeth "Betsy" Patterson, she of independent mind and immense ability, who did not, in fact, think much of her native city or the United States in general but preferred Europe. Her story has been told inaccurately in several novels and movies and more truthfully in a series of biographies, most recently, Charlene M. Boyer Lewis's *Elizabeth Patterson Bonaparte: An American Aristocrat in the New Republic* (Philadelphia: University of Pennsylvania Press, 2014), and three books published by the Maryland Historical Society. Claude Bourguignon-Frassetto's *Betsy Bonaparte: The Belle of Baltimore* (2002), originally published in France, is the portrait of an ingénue as seen through French eyes; Helen Jean Burn's *Betsy Bonaparte* (2010) concentrates on her subject's marriage to Napoleon's young brother and its aftermath, and Alexandra Deutsch's *A Woman of Two Worlds: Elizabeth Patterson Bonaparte* uses material culture to reveal the important and long-overlooked story of her later life. The story presented here, "Mr. Smith's Ball," draws upon these and quotes from Margaret Law Callcott, ed., *Mistress of Riversdale: The Plantation Letters of Rosalie Stier Calvert, 1795–1821* (Baltimore: Johns Hopkins University Press, 1991), 77–79.

The six-decades-long conflict between France and Britain, marked at one end by the Seven Years' War and on the other by what we know as the War of 1812, involved Maryland only peripherally in its early stages—the French and Indian War and the American Revolution—but the state was hardly so lucky as the continental wars roared on. Although many Americans were eager for war in 1812 and cast acquisitive eyes on Canada, which they regarded as ripe for the picking, that was not true of all. In "The Most Hated Man in Maryland," we have presented the story of Alexander Contee Hanson, James Madison's inveterate foe, as recounted in Frank A. Cassell, "The Great Baltimore Riot of 1812," *Maryland Historical Magazine* 70 (1975): 241–59.

Once declared, war soon came to Maryland by way of the Chesapeake Bay. Admiral George Cockburn, a swiftly rising star of the Royal Navy and a consummate villain, conducted devastating raids along the coastline that made him "The Scourge of the Chesapeake." See Christopher T. George, *Terror on the Chesapeake: The War of 1812 on the Bay* (Shippensburg, PA: White Mane Books, 2000); James Pack, *The Man Who Burned the White House: Admiral Sir George Cockburn, 1772–1853* (Emsworth, UK: Kenneth Mason, 1987); and Roger Morriss, *Cockburn and the British Navy in Transition: Admiral Sir George Cockburn, 1772–1853* (Columbia: University of South Carolina Press, 1997). The last days of Captain Peter Parker, one of Cockburn's protégés, are here recounted in "A Frolic with the Yankees," with material from Benson John Lossing, *The Pictorial Field Book of the War of 1812* (New York: Harper and Bros., 1868). For "The Cool Hand and the Hothead," I relied upon Christopher T. George, *Terror on the Chesapeake,* though a great many other books have been written about the burning of Washington. Especially enjoyable are Walter Lord's classic *The Dawn's Early Light* and Anthony Pitch's more recent *The Burning of Washington* (Annapolis, MD: Naval Institute Press, 1998). "Defenders," a recounting of the Battle of Baltimore, drew upon George, *Terror on the Chesapeake,* but accounts of that battle abound. For "The Chasseur," I owe a debt of gratitude to Scott S. Sheads, then a park ranger at the Fort McHenry National Historic Site, who provided much in the way of hard-to-find material, and Fred W. Hopkins Jr., *Tom Boyle: Master Privateer* (Cambridge, MD: Tidewater, 1976). Robert G. Stewart's "The Battle of the Ice Mound, February 7, 1815," *Maryland Historical Magazine* 70 (1975): 372–78, brought to light an otherwise forgotten episode that took place after peace had been signed but before the news reached Dorchester County.

The years between 1814 and 1861 were largely occupied with the issue of slavery in Maryland and elsewhere. As we consider removing all statues of Roger B. Taney, "Jacob Gruber" (drawn from Carl Brent Swisher, *Roger B. Taney* [New York: Macmillan, 1936]) reminds us that the author of the infamous Dred Scott decision should not be dismissed or dismantled so swiftly. Frederick Douglass ("The Slave-Breaker") wrote three slightly differing versions of his autobiography that William S. McFeeley has measured in *Frederick Douglass* (New York: W. W. Norton, 1991). And Harriet Tubman ("Moses") is demythologized and humanized in Kate Clifford Larson's excellent *Bound for the Promised Land: Harriet Tubman—Portrait of an American Hero* (New York: One World/Ballantine, 2004). One story that had until recently received little attention is that of freed slaves who traveled to the Maryland colony in Liberia. That lapse has been corrected in Richard L. Hall's *On Afric's Shore: A History of Maryland in Liberia, 1834–1857* (Baltimore: Maryland Historical Society, 2003), a thorough study drawn from the records of the Maryland Colonization Society that describes the grisly practice of "gidu." That slavery would come to a violent end was foreshadowed by the events described in "Christiana." The full story of that

1851 riot in Pennsylvania is to be found in Thomas P. Slaughter, *Bloody Dawn: The Christiana Riot and Racial Violence in the Antebellum North* (New York: Oxford University Press, 1991).

Of course, there was more to the antebellum years than the fight over slavery. "The Bear" derived from David M. Dean's article, "Meshach Browning: Bear Hunter of Allegany County, 1781–1859," in the *Maryland Historical Magazine* 91 (1996): 73–84, supplemented by Browning's own account as laid out in *Forty-four years of the Life of a Hunter: Being Reminiscences of Meshach Browning, A Maryland Hunter, roughly written down by himself,* revised and illustrated by E. Stabler (Philadelphia: Lippincott, 1859). On a lighter note, the half-comic history of Maryland's state sport ("The Vineyard Tournament") is to be found in G. Harrison Orians, "The Origins of the Ring Tournament in the United States," *Maryland Historical Magazine* 36 (1941): 263–77. "The Rose of Westminster" owes to numerous biographies of Poe.

No single individual can be credited with bringing on the Civil War, but John Brown would gladly have assumed that mantle had he been able. His story, from which I drew the details of his stoic ascent to the gallows, is ably told in Stephen B. Oates's *To Purge This Land with Blood: A Biography of John Brown* (New York: Harper and Row, 1970). Not to be lost in the myriad works arguing the importance of the riot of April 1861 in Baltimore is Frank Towers, ed., "Military Waif: A Sidelight on the Baltimore Riot of 19 April 1861," *Maryland Historical Magazine* 89 (1994): 427–46. The Union volunteer militia who were assaulted by pro-Southern sympathizers turned out to have been "Clara's Boys" at home in Massachusetts. The story of how the eventual founder of the Red Cross aided them when they reached Washington comes from Elizabeth Brown Pryor, *Clara Barton: Professional Angel* (Philadelphia: University of Pennsylvania Press, 1987), but see also Stephen B. Oates, *Woman of Valor: Clara Barton and the Civil War* (New York: Free Press, 1994). I discovered the story of the lonely mother who had lost one son in blue and another in gray ("Lost Sons") in George Alfred Townsend, *Rustics in Rebellion: A Yankee Reporter on the Road to Richmond, 1861–1865*, with an introduction by Lida Mayo (Chapel Hill: University of North Carolina Press, 1950). Far better known is Frederick, Maryland's, "Barbara Frietschie." Story and legend are untangled in Dorothy M. and William R. Quynn, "Barbara Frietschie," *Maryland Historical Magazine* 37 (1942): 227–54.

Life in Baltimore during the war was difficult for those whose sons and brothers went south to fight for the Confederacy and far better for the northern soldiers stationed in the camps surrounding the city. I drew "The Despot's Heel" from Kathryn Lerch's manuscript entitled "The Eighth New York Heavy Artillery," an account of the homesick upstate New York farm boys who manned the cannon on Federal Hill, overlooking the city. Their story would otherwise be unknown. Elements of "The Glorious Fourth . . . 1863" also came from the Lerch manuscript, from the *Baltimore Sun*, July 3–7, 1863, and from Garry Wills, *Lincoln at Gettysburg: The Words that Remade America* (New York: Simon and Schuster, 1992), whose pages also supplied details for "The Orator."

Edward G. Longacre's *A Regiment of Slaves: The 4th United States Colored Infantry, 1863–1866* (Mechanicsburg, PA: Stackpole Books, 2003) provided the basis for the story of that regiment's heroic contingent which is told in "Color Guard." "The Music of Point Lookout" drew details from Edwin W. Beitzell, *Point Lookout Prison Camp for Confederates* (published by the author, 1972); J. B. Traywick, "Prison Life at Point Lookout," *Southern Historical Society Papers* 18 (1891): 432; and Charles T. Loehr, "Point Lookout. Address before Pickett Camp Confederate Veterans, October 10, 1890, *Southern Historical Society Papers* 18 (1890): 116, all cited in Robert I. Cottom Jr. and Mary Ellen Hayward, *Maryland in the Civil War: A House Divided* (Baltimore: Maryland Historical Society, 1994), 104–7. The tragic story of "Hetty Cary" came courtesy of Prof. Cary Woodward, who supplied me with materials for this piece. "Ghosts of Western Maryland," which recounts the exploits of numerous Civil War spirits, came from *Tales of Mountain Maryland: With a Special Section on the C&O Canal* (iUniverse, 2005), a delightful little book by Paula M. Strain.

The "Gilded Age" that followed the Civil War was hardly gilded for most people. Tragedies—environmental and economic—followed hard on one another. "The Great Patapsco Flood of 1868" tells a story more fully chronicled in Henry K. Sharp's *The Patapsco River Valley: Cradle of the Industrial Revolution in Maryland* (Baltimore: Maryland Historical Society, 2001). The bases for "Early Racing at Pimlico" are found in Laura Rice's *Maryland History in Prints* (Maryland Historical Society, 2001). The tragedy behind the noble horse "Preakness" is available online at www.lambertcastle.org/preakness_race.html. Robert V. Bruce's lively *1877: Year of Violence* (Indianapolis: Bobbs-Merrill, 1959) describes "The Great Railroad Strike of 1877," but for quotes from the hard-pressed strikers, refer to the letters to Jno. King of the B&O Railroad, manuscript collection at the Maryland Historical Society. That things were not much better on the bay is evident in "Gus Rice," drawn from John R. Wennersten's colorful history, *The Oyster Wars of Chesapeake Bay* (Centreville, MD: Tidewater, 1981).

For those who could afford it, the Gilded Age certainly offered pleasures, sometimes to excess. As told in "The Maestro," the temperamental and often grouchy Peter Ilyich Tchaikovsky came to Baltimore in 1891. See James Morfit Mullen's "Tchaikowsky's Visit to Baltimore," *Maryland Historical Magazine* 34 (1939): 41–45. "Diamond Jim" Brady personified the hedonistic excess of the age (see H. Paul Jeffers, *Diamond Jim Brady: Prince of the Gilded Age* [New York: John Wiley and Sons, 2001]), but if these decades included gluttony, they were also a time of generous philanthropy in Baltimore. Enoch Pratt, George Peabody, and Johns Hopkins made life richer and healthier by creating a magnificent public library, the Peabody Institute, and the Johns Hopkins University. The story of several distinguished women who joined this all-male ensemble by endowing Hopkins medicine ("The Heiress and the Medical School") comes courtesy of Kathleen Waters Sander's biography, *Mary Elizabeth Garrett: Society and Philanthropy in the Gilded Age* (Baltimore: Johns Hopkins University Press, 2008).

For those who were not of the 1 percent, there was entertainment aplenty. African Americans, who suffered under segregation, lynching, and Jim Crow, created music that made spirits soar. "Mouse" is the story of one local musical genius who went on to national fame, Baltimore's Eubie Blake, whose biography by Al Rose, *Eubie Blake* (New York: Schirmer Books,

1979), is well worth reading. Of course, there was also baseball, in all its color, bawdiness, and drama. Witness "The Pennant," drawn from Burt Solomon's *Where They Ain't: The Fabled Life and Untimely Death of the Original Baltimore Orioles, the Team that Gave Birth to Modern Baseball* (New York: Free Press, 1999). "The Evil Empire," the rest of the country's name for the 1890s Orioles, draws from Bill Felber, *A Game of Brawl: The Orioles, the Beaneaters, and the Battle for the 1897 Pennant* (Lincoln: University of Nebraska Press, 2007), and James H. Bready, *Baseball in Baltimore: The First 100 Years* (Baltimore: Johns Hopkins University Press, 1998).

The fin de siècle almost brought with it the destruction of Maryland's greatest city. In 1904 a great fire swept through Baltimore's business district in thirty-six terrifying hours, leaving in its wake nothing but civic courage and indomitability, embodied in the story of "Goliath." Several histories of the fire are available, but I have mainly used Peter B. Peterson's *The Great Baltimore Fire* (Baltimore: Maryland Historical Society, 2004). As Baltimore rebuilt itself, the son of a Virginia couple who had moved there was challenging the oppressive economic order. With *The Jungle*, Upton Sinclair shocked the country by exposing the atrocious working conditions, not to mention the public health dangers, imposed by the "beef trust." "The Jungle" draws on his book as well as Anthony Arthur's *Radical Innocent: Upton Sinclair* (New York: Random House, 2006).

In the first decades of the new century, Americans, and some Europeans, thought they could conquer any obstacle, natural or man-made. "The Explorer" recounts how Matthew Henson accompanied Admiral Robert E. Peary on his quest to pinpoint the North Pole, only to find that his country's racial divide had accompanied the expedition. See Floyd Miller, *Ahdoolo: The Biography of Matthew Henson* (New York: Dutton, 1963). In 1910, celebrated French "aeronaut" Hubert Latham dazzled Baltimoreans by piloting his rickety biplane over the city. "The Aviator" is drawn from material supplied by the Maryland Historical Society's library staff and is available online at http://www.mdhs.org/underbelly/2013/03/07/antoin ette-in-the-air-hubert-latham-and-his-historic-flight-over -baltimore-1910/. Latham successfully challenged the air, but two short years later the "unsinkable" *Titanic* met disaster in the North Atlantic. That story, "Titanic," is drawn from Walter Lord, *A Night to Remember* (New York: Holt, Rinehart and Winston, 1955) and *The Night Lives On* (New York: William Morrow, 1986). The site https://www.encyclopedia-titan ica.org/titanic-survivor/lucile-polk-carter.html supplies the initial inaccurate newspaper reports of Lucy Carter and the sinking of the *Titanic*. This age of hope and confidence came to a bloody and much more tragic end with the First World War. "The Last Man," the story of Baltimore's Henry Gunther, was extensively reported in the newspapers, but I have drawn from Joseph E. Persico, *Eleventh Month, Eleventh Day, Eleventh Hour: Armistice Day, 1918, World War I and Its Violent Climax* (New York: Random House, 2004).

One irrepressible product of this period, who fittingly enlivened the "Jazz Age" that followed the war, was journalist, editor, and national scourge H. L. Mencken. In 1917, Mencken amused himself by hoodwinking the entire country with "The Great Bathtub Hoax," a piece contained in Mencken, *A Mencken Chrestomathy: His Own Selection of his Choicest*

Writings (New York: Vintage, 1982). His well-known opposition to Prohibition ("Maryland, the Free State") is described in Marion Elizabeth Rodgers, *Mencken: The American Iconoclast: The Life and Times of the Bad Boy of Baltimore* (New York: Oxford University Press, 2005). His duel with the Boston Watch and Ward Society, recounted in "Hatrack," draws on the same source, as well as from Fred Hobson's *Mencken: A Life* (New York: Random House, 1994).

The Jazz Age provided ideas for any number of amusing stories. Susan Saint Sing's *The Wonder Crew: The Untold Story of a Coach, Navy Rowing, and Olympic Immortality* (New York: St. Martin's, 2008) was the source for "Leander." I drew "Cab and Thurgood" from Juan Williams, *Thurgood Marshall: American Revolutionary* (New York: Three Rivers, 1998), and "Wallis" from J. Bryan III and Charles J. V. Murphy, *The Windsor Story* (New York: William Morrow, 1979). Other stories came courtesy of friends and colleagues. "The Schneider Cup Race of 1925" came across my desk when Michael Gough generously shared his article "Doolittle Wins in Baltimore," published in *Airpower,* November 2005, and colleague Donna B. Shear organized "The Crack-up" from the wealth of material written about Scott and Zelda Fitzgerald. "King Kong" is based on material supplied by Wallace Shugg in "The Socialite Spy from Baltimore: Marguerite E. Harrison, 1918–1922," his (as yet) unpublished manuscript.

The two stories here from the Second World War are centered on the American Twenty-Ninth Division, which included men from Maryland, Virginia, and Pennsylvania until heavy casualties necessitated a great many replacements. The Twenty-Niners landed on Omaha Beach, an event nowhere better recounted than in Stephen E. Ambrose's *D-Day, June 6, 1944: The Climactic Battle of World War II* (New York: Simon and Schuster, 1994). For the next eleven months they suffered unbelievable sacrifice and hardship. One of the replacements was a Bronx-born son of Austrian immigrants, who left an astonishing memoir. Emil Willimetz, "From Normandy to the Roer: A Footsoldier's Unsentimental Account of Combat with the 29th Division," *Maryland Historical Magazine* 96 (2001): 185–220, is the source for "Canajoharie at the Gut."

For most Marylanders, the 1950s were a wonderful decade. The amusing story of "Tunnel Joe" Holmes, the only man to successfully dig his way out of the state penitentiary, was brought to my attention by Wallace Shugg in *A Monument to Good Intentions: The Story of the Maryland Penitentiary, 1804–1995* (Baltimore: Maryland Historical Society, 2000). In *America's Game: The Epic Story of How Pro Football Captured a Nation* (New York: Random House, 2004), Michael MacCambridge recounted how "Johnny U.," a scrawny castoff from the Pittsburgh Steelers, became the greatest quarterback to play the game and in the process led his team to the national championship ("The Greatest Football Game Ever Played"). See also Frank Gifford and Harry Waters, *The Whole Ten Yards* (New York: Random House, 1993), and John F. Steadman, *The Greatest Football Game Ever Played* (Press Box Publishers, 1988). Though less pleasant to contemplate, the work of Rachel Carson, who had moved to Silver Spring, was one of the decade's most important contributions. See Linda Lear, *Rachel Carson: Witness for Nature* (New York: Henry Holt, 1997).

Most of these stories, excepting those contributed by listeners, and many others, are readily available in libraries and bookstores. A great many are to be found in the magnificent resources of the Maryland Historical Society—its library, the *Maryland Historical Magazine*, and in books recently published by its press.